Forensic Storytelling and the Literary Roots of Early Modern Feminism

The writing of letters and the rise of the novel provided a way for some women to express themselves at a time when the all-male French Academy defined the very parameters of French literary acceptability and tradition. Women who were consigned to convents, workhouses or prisons were in most respects deprived of agency, yet many found ways to respond to the legal documents served against them. The letters and associated materials preserved in their legal files provide evidence that these women did not remain quiet, as they found means to resist authority. The forensic storytelling examined in this book supports the conclusion that the documents written in these constrained circumstances have both historical and literary merit and form the core of an understudied genre of literature.

Barbara Abrams is Professor of French and Women's and Gender Studies and is Chair of the Department of History, Language, and Global Culture at Suffolk University, Boston. Her academic work focuses on French literature of the Enlightenment and Women's and Gender Studies. Her recent publications include several articles on women's epistolary writing in eighteenth-century France, the Factum as Fiction, and a new critical focus on the novels of Marie-Madeleine Bonafon. Her previous books include a multigraph project titled *Reframing Rousseau's Le Lévite d'Ephraïm: The Hebrew Bible, Hospitality, and Modern Identity* (Oxford University Studies in the Enlightenment) and *Le Bizarre and Le Décousu in the Novels and Theoretical Works of Denis Diderot: How the Idea of Marginality Originated in Eighteenth-Century France*, which examines the background of our modern concept of marginality by focusing on Diderot's materialist philosophy.

Routledge Focus on Literature

Shakespeare and the Theater of Pity
Shawn Smith

Trauma, Memory and Silence of the Irish Woman in Contemporary Literature
Wounds of the Body and the Soul
Edited by Madalina Armie and Verónica Membrive

Rilke's Hands
An Essay on Gentleness
Harold Schweizer

Orality, Form, and Lyric Unity
Poetics of Michael Donaghy and Don Paterson
Beverley Nadin

Milton and Music
Seth Herbst

Forensic Storytelling and the Literary Roots of Early Modern Feminism
ReSisters
Barbara Abrams

For more information about this series, please visit: www.routledge.com/Routledge-Focus-on-Literature/book-series/RFLT

Forensic Storytelling and the Literary Roots of Early Modern Feminism

ReSisters

Barbara Abrams

NEW YORK AND LONDON

First published 2024
by Routledge
605 Third Avenue, New York, NY 10158

and by Routledge
4 Park Square, Milton Park, Abingdon, Oxon, OX14 4RN

Routledge is an imprint of the Taylor & Francis Group, an informa business

Library of Congress Cataloging-in-Publication Data
Names: Abrams, Barbara Lise, author.
Title: Forensic storytelling and the literary roots of early modern feminism : reSisters / Barbara Abrams.
Description: New York : Routledge, 2023. | Series: Routledge focus on literature | Includes bibliographical references and index. |
Contents: Forensic storytelling and antimonarchical epistolarity – Les causes célèbres, factum or fiction? or: “That’s what he said!” – Tanastès est Satan: authenticity and audacity in the writings of Marie-Madeleine Bonafon – Excess or success? the case of Mme Geneviève de Gravelle – “What’s in a name?”: The case of Angélique Schwab – Conclusion. |
Identifiers: LCCN 2023034915 (print) | LCCN 2023034916 (ebook) |
ISBN 9780367029173 (hardback) | ISBN 9781032632728 (paperback) |
ISBN 9780429001147 (ebook)
Subjects: LCSH: French letters–History and criticism. | French prose literature–Women authors–History and criticism. | French prose literature–18th century–History and criticism. | French authors–18th century–Correspondence–History and criticism. | French women authors–Correspondence–History and criticism. | French literature–Women authors–History and criticism. | Women and literature–France–History–18th century. | French letter writing–History–18th century. | Feminism.
Classification: LCC PQ711 .A27 2023 (print) | LCC PQ711 (ebook) |
DDC 846/.609033–dc23/eng/20230807
LC record available at https://lccn.loc.gov/2023034915
LC ebook record available at https://lccn.loc.gov/2023034916

ISBN: 9780367029173 (hbk)
ISBN: 9781032632728 (pbk)
ISBN: 9780429001147 (ebk)

DOI: 10.4324/9780429001147

Typeset in Times New Roman
by Newgen Publishing UK

Contents

Acknowledgments

Many people contributed to the writing of this book project over the years. I am most appreciative of the support I have received from the Center for Scholarly Development and the Women's and Gender Studies programs at Suffolk University, whose grants allowed me to pursue my research at the Bibliothèque de l'Arsenal in Paris.

I have greatly benefited from the fine studies published in recent years by historians and scholars, some of whom I had occasion to meet at the Bibliothèque de l'Arsenal, including Arlette Farge and Lisa Jane Graham. I wish to express my deep gratitude to the Head Librarian of the Bibliothèque de l'Arsenal, Claire Lesage, as well as to the staff of the Archives for their steadfast devotion to maintaining these collections and making them available to researchers such as myself, despite the challenges of flooding and the pandemic over the past few years.

I am especially grateful to Dena Goodman for encouraging me to continue this line of questioning, even though I am not an historian. Thank you to Hilary Bowman, who discussed and shared her doctoral research with me with great enthusiasm. I am always thankful for the fruitful discussions and support of my colleagues over the years, especially Jennifer Vanderheydan, Karen Sullivan, and Mira Morgenstern. My thanks are also due to Pat Reeve and Christophe Martin for reading my book proposal and for their encouragement. Thank you to Marley Balenger for being such a receptive and enthusiastic student of Women's and Gender Studies and for reminding me that this work really matters. I am forever indebted to Anna Pravdica, who edited and indexed my work with such care.

I acknowledge with the deepest gratitude the sustenance, support, and patience of my husband David Kudan. I also wish to thank my children and their spouses: Ari Kudan, Maria Codlin, Talia Kudan, and Alden Abad. I love you all; you are all my “favorites.” This book is dedicated to the memory of my mother: the indomitable ReSister, Naomi Abrams.

Preface

King Louis XV would use the *lettre de cachet*, a royal letter conveying royal authority, to place women in convents, workhouses, and prison. The king could write this special order to place anyone under arrest and confine them for an offensive action. The collection of letters featured here are from consigned women who became known for their subversion, overtly or inadvertently, all proving annoyances to the king.

This book's central aim is to look at the written production of women who were accused of various crimes and imprisoned or cloistered in mid-eighteenth-century France. In this study, I contextualize and interpret several letters and documents from and about consigned women. These women seemingly had very little autonomy, underscoring the importance of their writing as an emergent subgenre of eighteenth-century literature. These letters and documents were in large part direct and indirect reactions against King Louis XV and patriarchal rule.

Many women, some famous, some infamous, had *lettres de cachet* used against them. Many remained quiet; but in some instances, they wrote to their families, their lawyers, or the king, seeking any recourse they might have had. Sometimes, volumes of these letters were compiled as they sought to explain their situations or beg for release and freedom from their confines. Antimonarchical epistolarity—or letters and documents written against the king's authority—makes up the core of this study. By engaging with the forensic evidence offered by these written documents, this book uncovers the antimonarchical epistolarity present in the legal briefs of silenced women, exploring their quests for freedom of expression, voice, and agency.

Introduction

While historians have often noted a connection between the explosion of print and the erosion of royal authority, they have tended to treat questions of form and content separately in their analysis of written works. This study seeks to address these two elements concurrently and to include other dimensions of analysis. I bring to bear historical, sociological, literary-critical, and feminist perspectives as I examine forensic storytelling, by providing authentic materials and contextual grounding in eighteenth-century France, with the aim of offering a multi-dimensional and nuanced understanding to studies of French literature.

The eighteenth-century public was passionately interested in the legal case folios that were published at the time. Robert Darnton explains that reports of trials and lurid courtroom dramas that were made available to the French public garnered great popular interest. One way such information was disseminated was through nightly newsprint, often put together after the news had been "gathered."[1] Often people would spread news and gossip in cafés and salons. Remarking on the proliferation of all manner of written activity and oral communication of current events, especially how print journalism began to feed the prurient interest of the public by stirring up the emotions of the populace, Darnton writes:

> Like most oral phenomena, it has disappeared. But it left traces of its activity at nodal points where the spoken word was picked up by writing and, in some cases, diffused still further by print. Talking and writing, hearing, and reading, ran

DOI: 10.4324/9780429001147-1

> together and amplified each other in ways that spread information everywhere, although they have rarely been noticed by historians. The difficulty in studying this subject comes from a lack of documentation. With some luck, however, a researcher will come across a dossier.[2]

In fact, these legal briefs do exist, and along with their contents they help to shed light on deeper processes in society as a prelude to the Revolution.

The genesis of this study can be traced back to the original work of my doctoral dissertation many years ago at Columbia University. I had received a grant to work on my dissertation and to consult original letters and manuscripts in the archives at the Bibliothèque Nationale de Paris (Mazarin) rare manuscripts room. My work was focused on a particular chapter on the foundations of Diderot's epistolary novel *La Religieuse*.[3]

In researching the more well-known examples of these types of public scandal cases, including works such as Diderot's *La Religieuse*, it left a deep impression on me to realize how important it would be to further explore how Diderot's epistolary novel draws upon and fictionalizes the real-life experience of Marguerite Delamarre, and by extension, to delve more deeply into the legal briefs and fictional literature that inspired it.[4]

The relevant information on Marguerite Delamarre suggests that she is the role model for Diderot's fictional protagonist, Suzanne Simonin, of *La Religieuse*. The letters and legal documents surrounding her trial, especially the remarks of Joly de Fleury, remained in my thoughts as a constant reminder of the context of women forced into living situations against their will. Though the story was compelling, I did not get a chance to use all the material in my dissertation. I was convinced, however, that the words and writing of women who were consigned to convents, workhouses, and prisons could serve as the basis of a kind of resistance literature, that is forensic in nature since it is based on material evidence.

Literary publications then began to shift their focus onto current events and the activity of the courtroom, as more current events-oriented stories proved appealing to the prurient appetites of the reading public and their desire for sensationalist tales. The fiction created by these lawyers expanded and included adulterous women and women accused of debauchery, many of whom were relegated to convents, workhouses, and prisons. Masculinist forms of literary production, including *Les Lettres de Cachet, Les Mémoires Judiciares, Les Causes Célèbres,* and *Les Notes sur les Filles Gallantes,* all provide striking admission that women of all classes possessed very limited agency of expression and were exploited in the rewriting of their lives.

Within the confines of eighteenth-century French society, women of the upper classes were offered some degree of education. They were afforded this privilege in convent schools and at home to make them marriage-ready. Overall, women were precluded from entering larger, more literary circles, except as hostesses in salons and patronesses of the arts and literature. It is true that the rise of the novel provided a way for some educated women to express themselves through their writing, but the then all-male French Academy dictated and defined the parameters of French literary acceptability and tradition. It is therefore logical that women's writings produced in the context of their legal proceedings were not considered to contribute to the literary production of the time. Still, the power of this literature was appreciated by the lawyers of the era, who began a trend of using these documents as the basis of their gossip-fueled work, in fact, the interpretation of court proceedings became the popular literature we know as *Les Causes Célèbres.* Perhaps the attention these materials garnered also fueled the efforts of women to write and protest more by all means at their disposal.[5]

Later, I researched the files of Marie-Madeleine Bonafon in the Archives de la Bastille at the Bibliothèque de l'Arsenal in Paris. In 1745, Bonafon published a roman-à-clef, *Tanastès*, set in an imaginary royal court punctuated by fantastical acts and the sexual conquests of royal figures. This work caused a short-lived but significant scandal. Well before all the published copies were sold, Bonafon was imprisoned in the Bastille. She fell ill and used her fragile situation to be transferred to a convent. She was then confined to a cloister in Moulins for many years and eventually released for good behavior. While her novel and legal battles were the subject of some interest in her time, Bonafon was largely dismissed as a writer and generally thought of as a curious chambermaid rather than as a woman of letters. While Bonafon's accusers and current historians agree that *Tanastès* was inflammatory, it is only after reading her legal brief that modern readers may reliably conclude that she was truly seeking to threaten the king through her work. That she managed to escape the cruelest of punishments and only be confined to a convent is a testament to her talent as a strategist and writer. The rediscovery and afterlife of this small but pointed novel, and especially the writings surrounding the "*Bonafon Affaire*," are the focus of this forensic investigation.

While I studied the story of Bonafon, I was reminded again of the letters of Marguerite Delamarre and the important fact that she was not alone in her reaction to the king. There were many women who were consigned against their will to the convent, and many who wrote to the king and the police to protest this form of injustice. In examining many of the legal briefs, I noticed that in the files there were letters, playing cards, pieces of fabric, memoirs, and all manner of materials that allow one to piece together a story of the consigned individual.[6] I also learned that some women, like Glucka/Angélique Schwab, even asked the king to help them leave their families as a kind of protection against their decided fate. It occurred to me that these women's authentic stories have both literary and historical merit, especially when studied within a feminist framework.

A story of particular fascination is the case of a Jewish woman, Glucka Schwab (also spelled Schouabe in the sources), who in 1729 was sent to the convent of Les Nouvelles Catholiques. In that same year, several members of the Schwab family were involved in the famous "Schwab Affair" involving bankers, accusations of financial crimes, and legal responses colored by the reigning antisemitic attitudes of French society in Paris and Metz. The extant legal records indicate police files were opened on the same day for a certain Abraham, son of Jacob and a woman named Glucka, daughter of Ruben. There is much evidence to suggest that these cases are related and that Glucka herself initiated her conversion to Catholicism. Her name became Angélique, and the young woman remained in the convent after her conversion. Soon afterward Angélique contracts an illness from which she is not expected to survive. We can only speculate on Angélique's motives for conversion and her entry into the convent. Jewish women like Angélique had little agency in family and in society. Her motives for conversion, assuming she made this choice for herself, may have been to separate herself from her family, who was then embroiled in legal problems. While her sincere conversion cannot be ruled out, it seems more likely that hers was a calculated attempt to gain more control over her desperate situation of forced marriage and a great deal of antisemitism. In a sense, for Angélique and perhaps others in desperate circumstances, conversion to Catholicism and residence in a convent may have provided a modicum of control, support, and safety for women who were particularly vulnerable.

We often hear the expression "the squeaky wheel gets the grease." Geneviève de Gravelle came to be heard and seen by virtue of her constant letter writing, which called attention to her unjust treatment. Her story illustrates the invisibility experienced by many women in her time, especially those "of a certain age," who had very little control over their lives and fates. Here we look at one woman's effort to be seen by being heard. Her story is emblematic of the conditions of women, their agency, rights, and accessibility to resources and recourse in mid-eighteenth-century France.

As we delve into our subject, it is well to keep in mind that the purpose of this study is to address the following questions: 1) Why did society seek to silence vulnerable women and isolate them from society? 2) Can we retell their truths in a more authentic voice if we are to use the methods available to us, including that of a modern feminist lens? This study focuses on the writings of women who were confined and of those who wrote responses in protest (directly or indirectly) of their confinement. With the newer readings, and a deeper awareness of the context and its significance, the continuous redefinition of these literary studies is impacted by considering the actual production and object in their authentic context.

Notes

1 Robert Darnton, "Theatricality and Violence in Paris, 1788," filmed 17 March 2022 at the Sheldonian Theatre, Oxford, England, video, 55:29.

2 "Mademoiselle Bonafon and the Private Life of Louis XV: Communication Circuits in Eighteenth-Century France," *Représentations* 87, no. 1 (2004): 103.

3 This work became my book, *Le Bizarre and Le Décousu in the Novels and Theoretical Works of Denis Diderot: How the Idea of Marginality Originated in Eighteenth-Century France* (Edwin Mellen Press, 2009).

4 Georges May performed the preliminary research on *La Religieuse* in his seminal work, *Diderot et "La Religieuse": Étude Historique et Littéraire* (New Haven: Yale University Press, 1954).

5 The *lettres de cachet* are a catalyst for creating a larger category of rhetoric and literature in eighteenth-century France and most specifically *Les Causes Célèbres*. The *lettres de cachet* are discussed in detail in the next chapters.
6 Reading through all the files in alphabetical order, I noted the top front page of each *memoire* that had a categorization of case "type." I also checked the uncategorized folios to make sure there were no letters penned by or dictated by women.

References

Abrams, Barbara. *Le Bizarre and Le Décousu in the Novels and Theoretical Works of Denis Diderot: How the Idea of Marginality Originated in Eighteenth-Century France.* Edwin Mellen Press, 2009.

Cixous, Hélène. "The Laugh of the Medusa." Translated by Keith Cohen and Paula Cohen. *Signs* 1, no. 4 (1976): 875–93.

Darnton, Robert. "Theatricality and Violence in Paris, 1788." Filmed 17 March 2022 at the Sheldonian Theatre, Oxford, England. Video, 55:29. www.voltaire.ox.ac.uk/event/professor-robert-darnton-theatricality-and-violence-in-paris-1788/

Darnton, Robert. "Mademoiselle Bonafon and the Private Life of Louis XV: Communication Circuits in Eighteenth-Century France." *Représentations* 87, no. 1 (2004): 102–124.

May, Georges. *Diderot et "La Religieuse": Étude Historique et Littéraire.* New Haven: Yale University Press, 1954.

1 Forensic Storytelling and Antimonarchical Epistolarity

Women, Equality, Liberty: Private Lives and Public Spheres, 1715–1815

A recent lecture about feminist literary studies in France, which emerged from a long-term study group on *Femmes littéraires* at Harvard University, proposes to reverse the paradigm of a male-dominated definition of "what makes a piece literary."[1] This project, under the directorship of Christie MacDonald, sought to define the many different categories of women's writing in France in the eighteenth century. This study group brought together many scholars and graduate students working in eighteenth-century and women's and gender studies and employed a new tool for their investigations: the search engine at the Bibliothèque Nationale de France. This powerful system, paired with the resources of the research group and a vast database, made it possible to trace the history of women's literature and the evolution of ideas therein by searching the following terms over time: *libertés, égalités, dilemmes.* MacDonald begins the study by seeking to clarify what is meant by *liberté* from a feminist perspective. With further precision, the researchers posed the question, "What was the experience of women as writers and how did they see their intellectual, social, and political roles?" It is through this lens that MacDonald questions how women in the eighteenth century approached written discourse. The last part of the study proposes several ways to think about the history of literature and women's role in shaping literature in general. The key, according to MacDonald, is to identify the form of the conflicts or tensions that female authors brought to the genre itself. These she would refer to as the *dilemmes*. Chief

DOI: 10.4324/9780429001147-2

among the *dilemmes* reflected in women's writing of the period is the conflict between duty to the patriarchy and the powerful desire to be free from it.

Characteristic of the literary expressions in this category were the writings of Olympe de Gouges. De Gouges' theatrical and political-philosophical treatises were her main literary forms of expression, and these choices speak volumes. She eschewed softer, more "feminine" forms of writing to express her political views, and therefore even her choice of literary form challenged patriarchal rule. Much of her writing looks at the foundations of human rights and is feminist in its focus; some of her work collides with Enlightenment principles. Though De Gouges mainly engaged in epistolary writing, she garnered much more attention for her radical literature, such as *La Déclaration des Droits de la Femme et des Citoyennes*. Epistolary writing, especially by women, is still the focus of much debate in defining and appraising literary quality, and it provides scaffolding for the following study.

The novel form itself was in its infancy and was viewed as a particularly feminine form of expression. Educated women could write, though oftentimes not well, because their education did not match their writing skills. Nevertheless, they could read and talk of intrigue and passion.[2] Though more masculine forms of novel writing were being developed in England by Richardson and Fielding, the novel was still principally a feminine form of writing in eighteenth-century France, and the readership was largely female. The role of the novel is referred to in the factum containing letters to Joly de Fleury as early as 1729: "When you will learn of it, there will no longer be the danger of confiding the smallest secret to the heroine of such a novel."[3] Even Fleury understood the so-called "feminine" attractions and qualities of novels.

Letter writing was a skill taught to women to be employed for domestic and social purposes. Not surprisingly, letters of the period often associated women with feeling and men with reason, and this idea correlated with the divergent educations afforded to men and women. However, by the second half of the century, a new binary distinction arose between two different forms of rhetoric: masculine oratorical eloquence and feminine epistolary style, the latter of which was linked to orality, especially through the salons. For women, conversation and correspondence proved to be "wit" with words. For educated women, letter writing had become an essential discipline in the seventeenth century, and this trend would evolve in the eighteenth century. For women, the act of writing became increasingly important as access to education increased. This book looks at the expansion of women's expression and a particular kind of letter writing as political and feminist modes of expression.

Letters often served as an extension of conversation and reflected the discussions of the salon. Letter writing falls somewhere between speech and more formal writing: "Defined as conversation with someone who is absent, it was ordinary language simply placed on the page; it was writing the way one speaks."[4] In other words, letters were used as a sort of supplement to formal speech. Some women seemed to establish an epistolary dependency, and certainly when there was no other recourse, writing was especially significant. In this case, there is often a connection with the body of the letter, and on occasion the writing becomes harsh and fervent. The writing of letters can be symbolic in all its gestures and could not be translated to another medium of writing. In the file briefs, women's letters were not conformist letters, glorifying privilege not the women's class at the time; rather these letters were full of resistance against the patriarchal authority of the king. Perhaps at times letter writing betrayed passive-aggressive formulations of language. Women writers skillfully employed tropes that would bring them closer to their goal of challenging the authority that consigned them to the convent or prison.

Dena Goodman identifies the goal of the writer of letters in the eighteenth century to compose in a style that "ought to make its negligence felt and not differ at all from ordinary language."[5] On women and letter writing, Goodman describes a "naturalness of letter writing and its importance of friendship rather than relations of patronage."[6] Women were identified as natural letter writers and that is why male authors appropriated this style and used the voice of women when they wrote their epistolary novels. One need only cite Jean-Jacques Rousseau, whose cloistered Julie in *La Nouvelle Heloise* receives the remark: "My Julie, how touching is the simplicity of your letter!"[7]

Epistolary writing began to stand apart as a form of literature as people used the tools they had honed in other contexts, such as the café and the salon. Letter writing evolved into a new genre to respond to multiple social and intellectual needs. The letters we examine in this book are often full of formulaic polite phrases that respond to the royal letters that impinged upon their freedoms and privileges. As we seek to study and understand women's responses to King Louis XV and his agents, one central question must be addressed: what was the relationship of epistolarity to the political and personal act of writing for women who were consigned against their will to the convent or, even worse, relegated to prisons?

Forensic storytelling is the act of telling a story that is carved from real-life experience using objects and materials from the past to assist in the narration. It is a narrative that expresses the subjective quality of truth from the perspective of the researcher. Forensic storytelling is first and foremost the sharing of experiences by way of materiality and authenticity. It often requires seeking evidence or testimony that is key to survival, in this case: the archives and legal briefs.

When reading a story that conveys forensic qualities, one may consider the historiography, the psychology, and the quality of testimony of the objects, materials, and the narrative. This type of storytelling is not separate nor mutually exclusive of other types of storytelling, but it is an important strategy in the consideration of this genre. In seeking to establish the writings of women as "literary" from a modern feminist perspective, the issues of testimony, argument, credibility, reconciliation, and historicity, all lead to the idea that there is a coherence in writing and specifically in the writing of letters linked to the epistolary style of eighteenth-century France. The men who provided the evidence, such as the lawyers, the police, and even the king, are all participants in the process of forensic storytelling.

Forensic storytelling in the eighteenth century specifically derives from the newly found freedom of literacy and draws heavily from letter writing and later contributes largely to the development of the novel as a literary genre. This type of storytelling finds its richness in the stories recounted by women in prison, workhouses, and the convent. It is the collection of stories based on truths that weave a tale and attempt to recount it for posterity.

Male authors often expropriated the work of women. According to Elisabeth Wingrove: "Much of women's writing was considered improper, chaotic, and uncontainable."[8] Much of the literary production of women in the eighteenth century can be said to express vulnerability, and this contributed to this literature having been criticized for its lack of literary quality.

> From this perspective, a literary approach helpfully turns us away from a historical linguistic structure to see, perhaps to hear, a discursive word giving shape to political possibilities. It likewise turns us away from the transhistorical expressive subject to consider instead the simultaneously rhetorical, material, and institutional resources through which "voice" is both crafted and denied.[9]

Forensic evidence provides researchers with a way to piece together the stories that are told by people through evidence and by writing their own stories in the past. It helps to narrate the history of the literature one is reading. Jacques Rancière argues, "History is sacrificed to historiography, which in its scientific and managerial aspirations becomes a division of political science."[10] In addition, he insists on exploring the simultaneously methodological, political, and aesthetic stakes that are at the base of literary interpretation. Rancière suggests that using letters as evidence in the eighteenth century precludes our ability to "hear the poor," or those who may not have had access to writing. It also decides who gets to count, or what he refers to as "the partition of the sensible."[11] While it is true that the poor and illiterate did not have the chance to write and record their stories, the scribes and lawyers often told the tale for them in the legal brief. Therefore, studying the factum gives greater access to the forensic approach and would help both literary critics and historians understand critical dynamics, among them ideas of class.

Literary analysis of letters and objects from the past poses many problems, presenting recurring sensory and ontological challenges. One fascinating example of forensic reading is Elizabeth Wingrove's essay on the letters of Geneviève de Gravelle, which is discussed in a later chapter. Wingrove helps to bring together different types of forensic knowledge; using letters and testimony she produces a reconsideration of literary interpretation that pays close attention to prose content and form and how language articulates human relations in the past. Wingrove takes a close look at the legal brief and the objects that provide testimony to Gravelle's life. Wingrove demonstrates how the letter, at once expressive and strategic, material and rhetorical, engendered new opportunities for political contestation on the part of speakers who would not otherwise have the chance to come forward. Wingrove concludes that "Gravelle's untimely and ungrammatical excess of words challenged sovereignty just by existing." The question here is how we can differentiate between fiction and fact, and how we can avoid the confabulation or fictionalization that naturally occurs in this type of reading, especially when linked with the legal cases?

The actual letters, in the legal files without re-interpretation or embellishment, hold powerful stories of their own.[12] The enactment of such a resistance letter showed tremendous authorial power. It was often difficult to find the materials to construct the letter, let alone imagine how it would ever arrive at its destination. The authors were all considered illegitimate, as the letters they sent were not solicited (recall that the *lettre de cachet* did not require or anticipate a response, and in fact declared the *destinataire* illegitimate).[13]

The *salonnières* were instrumental in eighteenth-century France in the development of the epistolary novel form. This genre emerged from a feminine social context. This is natural as letter writing in the context of eighteenth-century France was considered a binarily female type of communication. Mme de Tencin, Mme de Geoffrin, Mme de Genlis, Mme de Graffigny, and Mme Riccoboni all contributed significantly to the development of the Enlightenment as hostesses of their salons, while as memoir and letter writers they also contributed to the style of the novel. Indeed, the epistolary form is a central incarnation of this literary exploration. It is certainly the case that many authors in the eighteenth century derived their epistolary stories from actual correspondence. Their real-life letters provided grist and inspiration for the epistolary novel form as an especially efficient, convenient, and accessible form of expression. One might almost say it was a "stealth" form of novel writing, as it could be judged in different ways and was less threatening to a male-dominated readership and the philosophical public. Letters were at the core of writing and therefore of literature in eighteenth-century France.

It has been established that the salons served a key role in establishing a transitional space between the private and public sphere for women in the eighteenth century and earlier. The salon served as a setting in which women could learn, digest, and provide feedback on intellectual content from the private sphere and interact within the public sphere through the commentary and discussion that ensued within the confines of their estates. In her early work on the salons, Dena Goodman demonstrates how the salon served as a base and a network for communication: "The *philosophes* found an institutional base in this institution, especially in the Parisian salon."[14] The salon was a site of gendered educational exchange between men and women even as it was a site of sexual encounters.[15] Élisabeth Badinter contends that while men in eighteenth-century France may have thought that women sought fame and ambition in the salons, women were there to learn and instruct, and in fact fame and ambition were looked at as dubious qualities in a woman.[16] Characterizing women's motivations in this way may be seen as a way of discounting women's agency and ability in a very significant cultural enterprise.

The salons of seventeenth-century France were more social and stratified than those of the eighteenth century. In the seventeenth century, they were viewed as places for social gatherings and promoted as *les passe-temps* or ways for the leisure class to spend their time. Often during the *ancien régime*, people who attended a salon would play social games, promote word games and rhetorical discourse, or even gamble at cards or *jeux de société*. What distinguishes the eighteenth-century salon from that of the *ancien régime* is the evolving notion of leisure time. There was a purposefulness to the eighteenth-century salon that evolved over time and specifically during the Enlightenment. The Enlightenment salon placed an emphasis on writing, poetry, literature, philosophy, music, art, and sometimes the reading of well-written letters. Women played a central role in transforming the salon of the seventeenth century into a true Enlightenment institution. There was a new spirit of collaboration, and the salons became centers where philosophical discourse took place. and art and literary criticism developed. Much of the discourse was of a philosophical and literary nature, and the salon eventually became a setting for politically charged exchanges.

The *esprit critique* that animated so many of these gatherings also encouraged the promotion of social equality among cultivated people. Thus, the bourgeoisie and aristocrats were on a more equal footing in the atmosphere of the salon. This issue of equality was also applied to women, particularly in the Enlightenment salon. Yet in post-revolutionary France, the ideals of the Enlightenment salon were much diminished as the ideals of the *luminaires* were obscured. The nineteenth-century salon that was to follow the French Revolution reverted to its earlier, more social function, placing a high value on social status. These salons and the women who led them actively asserted the idea that nobility could be acquired through education and sophistication, and that the *salonnières* were instrumental in facilitating this transformation.[17] The Enlightenment *salonnières* employed their considerable talents, and chief among them was typically a penchant for organization, and determination to achieve their ends. Being a good *salonnière* was a significant achievement and a mark of status.[18]

To become a successful *salonnière* one required training and preparation. It was important later in the eighteenth century for women of the salon to have their education supervised by older and more experienced *salonnières*. Such was the case for Mme de Tencin who would become the mentor for the most renowned salon in Paris during the Enlightenment. Her disciple was none other than Mme de Geoffrin, later the host of the most active intellectuals of the Enlightenment.

Diderot and D'Alembert strategically promoted their own ideas under the auspices of the Enlightenment salon through their friendship with Julie de L'Espinasse. At the time it was thought that it would be desirable to have an Enlightenment-philosophy-focused salon that was promoted by a woman. L'Espinasse was the ideal host, embodying the ethos of women who were independent thinkers. She organized salons that catered directly to the *philosophes*. L'Espinasse and her circle were also active in expressing themselves through the writing of letters.[19] The epistolary exchange became all-important. "Not people nor letters but the principles that underlay their social and intellectual principles of reciprocity are the center of the Enlightenment Philosophy."[20]

Not all *philosophes* were in favor of the expanding role of the salon. In 1758, Rousseau pronounced his denunciation of *salonnières* in his *Lettre à M. d'Alembert sur son article "Genève*."[21] Rousseau commented on the developing seriousness of the salon by mentioning in his *Confessions*, in books seven and eight, that he began to feel threatened by the criticisms of these women, paradoxically giving this forum more weight than people had previously.[22]

He commented on the visibility and dominance of the *salonnière* as a type of "gender disorder" that results from decaying society and women turning to the salon.[23] In *Émile*, Rousseau asked: what is the "nature" of women?[24] His 1762 discussion centers on women's voice and capability to reason. The consideration of women writing to "*declarer des droits*," or declare their rights, and "*écrire pour louvoyer*," or write for tackling ideas, was a debate central to the *Émile*, as Rousseau maps out his program for women's education.

An interesting parallel may be seen between the salon and the convent. As with the salon, the convent served as a transitional space between the private and public spheres. Where the salon differed greatly was in the idea of sociability. Women attended and hosted salons as part of the public sphere. Convents offered very few "outward facing" possibilities, though the educational and auto-didactical possibilities increased for women behind the walls of the convent. Letters circulated through the convents just as they did in the salons. These letters often served very different functions and were a lifeline for women who possessed no other recourse. Convents often performed a moral and social function, and only secondarily a pedagogical one.[25] One problem in formative education is that parents did not necessarily want to educate their female children. This left many women after a poor convent education to become autodidacts.[26]

Modern readers have an acquaintance with French eighteenth-century convent life through *La Religieuse*, *Les Lettres Portugaises*, *Venus de la Clôitre*, and *Histories du Dom Bouge, ou le Portier Chartreux*. Unlike the salon, the convent was more equitable for women in terms of class, because women of all economic strata had access to the convent.[27] If there were disorder in the convent, it would endanger rights guaranteed to all subjects and undermine the authority of the magistrates of the sovereign courts.

The convent provided a liminal space between the home and the outside world.[28] The convent was seen as having both positive and negative aspects for women in the eighteenth century. Much of the epistolary fiction written by both men and women of the time derived from fictionalized realities. These fictions were often based on real letters written from the convent, some shocking and brutal, which won popularity by the very gruesomeness of their stories.[29] Other stories, when retold through fictional representation, had the power to portray the convent as a safe haven for women who might otherwise have been at the mercy of a spouse or family member.[30]

Not only Catholic women benefited from the possibility of being saved from a bad marriage by dedicating themselves to a life in the convent. Jansenists and Protestants, and some exceptional Jews, sought refuge from bad marital situations throughout the centuries by requesting haven in a convent.[31] In her article "Room to Grow: The Convent in Graffigny, Riccoboni and Gouges," Karen Sullivan describes the largely positive image painted by women authors regarding the role of the convent for eighteenth-century women.[32] She argues that scholars have also collected positive images that appear in novels, especially by women, promoting the benefits of women living in the convent. At the same time, we must confront the reality that many women were forced against their will to live in the convent, and some were even forced to take vows against their will. This latter phenomenon is the focus of this exploration.[33]

The king had at his fingertips a tool that he used to keep order and channel direct authority. This mechanism, the *lettre de cachet,* had many useful functions. This peculiar mechanism for making manifest the king's authority, especially over women, was directly connected to women's forensic literary expression. The king would choose a form of justice to execute according to his judgment; he would then have his will enacted through the chosen system. The work of Arlette Farge and Michel Foucault in *Le Désordre des familles* highlights the changes in the types of *lettres de cachet* from the beginning of the eighteenth century (1724) to mid-century (1760) and the direct correlations to the changes in family structure and values.[34] In *Le Désordre des familles*, Farge and Foucault discuss the *lettres de cachet* in terms of their predominant use by many citizens and the traditional understanding of their use by the monarchy. Farge and Foucault largely concentrate on the lives of people of the lower classes and emphasize that the letter was not necessarily a condemnation, but a correction for something considered an offense.[35] Their study has produced much information on women by way of statistics and context. Farge and Foucault argue that women's issues often represented not only "disorder" in the eighteenth-century family structure, but also in the *ancien régime.* Foucault notes that familial requests for a personal letter (*lettre de cachet*) from the king were considered a special form of "justice" that was higher than the law and was used to consign family members and especially women.[36] Oftentimes families would request these letters because they did not want their circumstances to go public, especially in cases of incest or debauchery.[37] The *lettres de cachet* increased around 1760, but curiously after this date the archival *lettres* are more difficult to find.[38]

Examples of the *lettres*' use as a repressive force figured centrally in the literature of eighteenth-century France.[39] The historical significance of the *lettres de cachet* to this particular study is that they epitomized the repression and indiscriminate imprisonment of various women who dared to revolt or even criticize the monarchy.[40] There was a direct political connection between the *lettres de cachet* and the collected letters and *mémoires* of confined women, which testifies to their attempts to be released from oppressive situations.[41] Patriarchal traditions of male power and the salic laws in France precluded women's autonomy, and women had little recourse in the face of the king's corrections and punishments. It seems that the *lettres de cachet* had a history of oppression, as Claude Quétel has argued, rather than the correctionist use that Farge and Foucault discussed earlier.[42]

Bourgeois and upper-class women did have at least one tool they could use in response to the king, which might soften royal decree.[43] This tool was a woman's literacy and her ability to write persuasive letters to rally support and evince sympathy and understanding. Learning how to read and write, even at a very basic level, could serve as a weapon, the impact of which has been overlooked. In addition to literacy, women knew how to network in ways that men did not; the salon proved to be fertile ground for the exercise of this specific skill. Of course, knowing where to address a letter to maximum effect would also have been crucial to achieving a positive outcome. Some women had specific connections to court, which would have assisted in their social and political networking. Women in general had less education and therefore weaker writing skills overall. This included poor spelling and grammar. Yet, some women demonstrated great skill in corresponding, responding, and even documenting their lives, especially the more educated and women of privilege.

Lisa Jane Graham has demonstrated the direct effect the letter had on a specific woman in the bourgeoisie and the aristocracy.[44]

Graham discusses the general behavioral codes of the upper classes and describes how women of a certain age and marital status were treated. She examines a very precise usage of the *lettres de cachet*.[45] Graham states: "By their very nature, the *lettres de cachet* were above the authority of the courts and subject to no other appeal than that of the king's benevolence in censorship of his own judgment."[46] Unintentionally, these letters form the base for "dialogic forensic storytelling." In other words, though they did not anticipate a response, they often elicited one by their very existence. Thus, the *lettres de cachet* were a catalyst for creating larger categories of rhetoric and literature in eighteenth-century France.[47] They became the subject and the object of much that was written.

Certain caveats must be acknowledged, though: the *lettre de cachet* was not meant to solicit a response, as it was a form of rhetoric that had a prescribed answer. It was *un ordre du roi* (a command from the king). As Elizabeth Wingrove says, the *lettre de cachet* produces "a vicious circularity and a productive paradox."[48] Historian Robert Darnton corroborates that when the *lettres de cachet* were outlawed in 1784, there was ample evidence that they were still in use.[49] Nevertheless, the *lettre de cachet* seems to have elicited, and even invited, written responses from the women whose lives it affected. *Familles* and Lisa Jane Graham in *Mystifying the Monarch* examines the usage of the *lettre de cachet* in eighteenth-century France as a tool used to control women who acted outside the expected norms.

The *Causes Célèbres*, which drew directly on the legal briefs that became known as the *Mémoires Judiciares*, became a popular form of literature in mid-eighteenth-century France. In this new kind of fiction, lawyers fictionalized case files, and contrasted images of aristocratic decadence with the simple lifestyle of an untitled family in order to elicit sympathy for their clients, using a trope of class conflict. These accounts, based on the struggles of real people, had the ring of authenticity and immediacy.[50] Much of the legal writing, whether dictated to scribes, secretaries or written directly by the lawyers, shed light on the ways in which female authority proved threatening in the cloister and the salon and beyond. In any case, women's influence through the various channels, including letter writing, seems to have been quite substantial. Of particular interest to lawyers and to those reading their arguments in popular literature were the lurid depictions of monastic despotism. This topic has been explored by Nadine Berenguier in her essay "Victorious Victims."[51] In her work she suggests that the *Mémoires Judiciares* display a complex negotiated process in which female agency was represented in the context of male subjectivity.[52] Berenguier explains how lawyers highlighted their female clients' reluctance to present their troubles to the public and turned the victorious women who often won their cases into victims of their fame and fate.

Denunciation of women's bad behavior, or *mauvaise conduite*, produced the basis for much gossip and interest by the public in reading legal briefs as a distraction. At this point in history, the factum, and the *Causes Célèbres* become a form of forensic storytelling. Women often reacted by writing letters to lawyers, loved ones, and their inner networks in order to call the king's authority into question when they were assigned a *lettre de cachet*. In some files, women wrote directly to the king himself. These letters and responses reflected an enactment of agency and an expression of self. In this sense, the letters were antimonarchical. The very ink that was used, the paper, the tears that fell onto the page, the wax on the seal—all inform a forensic literary approach.[53]

When one asks whether literature is privately or publicly directed, the question becomes: to whom was the writing addressed? Who was the target and audience? Epistolarity generally answers this question by being addressed to someone. But, paradoxically in the case of a *lettre de cachet* or a *mémoire* or a legal brief, this was not necessarily the case, making its reading even more nuanced. The letter engendered new opportunities for women for political contestation and resistance and sometimes in this form of writing, expresses the writer's sense of dislocation and chaos. There is a continuous search for coherence on the part of the author, and the reader is employed in assembling the bits and pieces of the story. It is a kind of reading that takes effort, as well as patience, sympathy, and curiosity. Many of the letters reflect what came into the writer's head at the time; they reflect an attempt at a dialog, or sometimes just self-reflection. In other words, it is often difficult to determine the assumed destination, or "*destinataire*," of the missive. This is not literature that is readily available to any reader. As Wingrove states, "These are practices that cannot be read through authorial intention."[54]

The aim of looking at these files is to shift some of these barriers, help tell these stories, and make them more accessible. The suffering one reads and understands when deciphering these letters becomes intelligible as an ongoing act of resistance, as Wingrove terms as "cries of pain becoming an act of justice only in so far as one can claim a place in political dialogue."[55] So the question remains: how does this voice act as a multiply mediated event whose audibility might be precarious? This question prompts me to make these letters as audible and readable as possible. As with many of the letters contained in the legal brief, there is no anticipation of a response. Especially in some of the cases, this conjures the idea of perpetual self-address or a kind of outlet for emotional expression for some.

Joan Landes has illuminated the ways women were relegated to domestic and private spheres in eighteenth-century France, while men were an active part of public and political spheres. These sociopolitical lines continued to develop long past the eighteenth century and were especially promoted by the philosophy of Rousseau in *Émile*. Despite the sense of purpose that many women maintained they had gained through Rousseau's writing, there was still a yearning for participation and agency in the political sphere. Another in-between place could be within the margins of the letter. As Dena Goodman has described in her book *Becoming a Woman in the Age of Letters*, letter writing was a means for women to cultivate a space that was simultaneously private and public, as it was constructed inwardly but directed outwardly.[56]

The next section of this book treats the complex relationships between factual and fictional literature. As we move forward, we will explore the following assemblage of pieces: the letters, *mémoires*, legal briefs, and factum, which illustrate the rhetorical repertoire that was available to each consignee. In addition, the files demonstrate how court gossip and unsolicited responses act as catalysts for creating a broader category of rhetoric and literature in eighteenth-century France. We will begin by examining the trial records recreated by lawyers in romanticized and fictionalized versions of female voices in the *Causes Célèbres*, and then move on to an examination of authentic female voices in the case studies of Marie-Madeleine Bonafon, Geneviève de Gravelle, and Angélique Schwab.

Notes

1 Christie McDonald, "Mapping the Strategies for the 18th Century Section of *Femmes, littérature. Une histoire culturelle* (in progress): *libertés, égalités, dilemmes*," (lecture, Mahindra Humanities Center, Harvard University, 1 February 2017), https://complit.fas.harvard.edu/event/mapping-strategies-18th-century-section-femmes-littérature-une-histoire-culturelle.

2 "As royal historiographers recorded the exploits of the Sun King for posterity, an alternative script took shape in the hands of authors experimenting with a fictional technique called the novel. Blending the traditions of epic and romance with current events, novels probed the human heart and developed a language to express the role of the emotions in human behavior. This endeavor fleshed out the individual but also revealed the limits of reason as a guide to character. By elaborating a subjective language of interiority, novelists subverted the crown's hegemony on culture and taste. They also challenged principles of privilege and hierarchy that structured Ancient Regime society and government. Ironically, as character acquired greater sophistication in eighteenth-century literature, it undermined a coherent understanding of the self. This development threatened classical conceptions of royal character and the theories of rule that shaped it." Lisa Jane Graham, "Fiction, Kingship and the Politics of Character in Eighteenth-Century France," in *Mystifying the Monarch: Studies on Discourse, Power, and History*, eds. Jeroen Deploige and Gita Deneckere (Amsterdam: Amsterdam University Press, 2006), 140.

3 "*Quand vous le saurez qu'il n'y ait beaucoup de danger à confier le moindre secret à l'héroïne d'un pareil roman.*" M. Gamaras to Cardinal de Fleury. Paris, Archives de la Bastille (AB), MS 11072, 74. All translations by the author unless otherwise stated.

4 Dena Goodman, *Becoming a Women in the Age of Letters* (Ithaca: Cornell University Press, 2009), 139.

5 Ibid., 140.

6 For further discussion of Laclos, Rousseau, and Diderot see ibid., 143.

7 *La Nouvelle Héloïse* in *Oeuvres* Complètes, eds. Bernard Gagnebin and Marcel Raymond, vol. 2 (Paris: Bibliothèque de la Pléiade, Gallimard, 1961), part 1, letter 12, 77-79.

8 Elizabeth Wingrove, "Sovereign Address," *Political Theory* 40, no. 2 (2012): 138.

9 Ibid.

10 Jacques Rancière, *The Names of History: On the Poetics of Knowledge*, trans. Hassan Melehy (Minneapolis: University of Minnesota Press, 1994), 35, 41.

11 Jacques Rancière, *The Politics of Aesthetics*, trans. Gabriel Rockhill (London: Continuum, 2006), 12-19.
12 These letters (especially in the cases of women denied access to paper and pen, like Gravelle and Bonafon) could be classified as illicit.
13 Elizabeth J. MacArthur makes comments on women's writing style in her discussion of La Bruyère. She cites his example: "*Ce sexe va plus loin que le nôtre dans ce genre d'écrire…Si les femmes étaient toujours correctes, j'oserais dire que les lettres de quelques unes d'entre elles seraient peut-être ce que nous avons dans notre langue de mieux écrit.*" "Devious Narratives: Refusal of Closure in Two Eighteenth-Century Epistolary Novels." *Eighteenth-Century Studies* 21, no. 1 (1987): 18, see also footnote 27.
14 Dena Goodman, "Enlightenment Salons: The Convergence of Female and Philosophic Ambitions," *Eighteenth-Century Studies* 22, no. 3 (1989): 329–50.
15 Goodman, *Becoming a Woman*, 14.
16 Élisabeth Badinter, *Émilie, Émilie: L'ambition féminine au 18ième siècle* (Paris: Flammarion, 1983).
17 This discussion is informed by Dena Goodman's treatment of the *salonnières* in *The Republic of Letters: A Cultural History of the French Enlightenment* (Ithaca: Cornell University Press, 1994), 74-75.
18 "This discussion is also linked to the idea that Diderot put forth of 'politesse' and is indirectly linked to developing notions of hospitality in the eighteenth century, which were also problematic for Rousseau." Barbara Abrams, "Decoding Hospitality: Image and Polity in Rousseau's *Lévite d'Ephraïm*," in *Reframing Rousseau's Lévite D'Ephraïm: The Hebrew Bible, Hospitality, and Modern Identity* (Liverpool University Press, 2021), 125.
19 Goodman speaks of L'Espinasse and her important relationships with the *philosophes* in the salon. *Republic of Letters*, 222-224.
20 Ibid., 342.
21 *Politics and the Arts: Letter to D'Alembert on the Theatre*, ed. and trans. Alan Bloom (Ithaca: Cornell University Press, 1964), 4.
22 Rousseau has several prolonged discussions about his anxiety with women in *Les Confessions* in *Oeuvres Complètes*, eds. Bernard Gagnebin and Marcel Raymond, vol. 1 (Paris: Bibliothèque de la Pléiade, Gallimard, 1959), books 7-8.
23 "The most esteemed woman is the one who has the greatest renown, about whom the most is said, who is the most often seen in society, at one's home who dines the most, who most imperiously sets the time, who judges, who resolves, decides, pronounces, assigns talents, merit, and virtues their degrees and places, and whose favor is most ignominiously begged for by humble, learned men…In society they do not

know anything but they judge everything." Rousseau, *Politics and the Arts: Letter to D'Alembert on the Theatre,* ed. and trans. Alan Bloom (Ithaca: Cornell University Press, 1964), 49.

24 *Émile* in *Oeuvres Complètes*, eds. Bernard Gagnebin and Marcel Raymond, vol. 4 (Paris: Bibliothèque de la Pléiade, Gallimard, 1969), book 1, 249.

25 Arlette Farge and Michel Foucault report that, in 1769, "*Le critère social 'à ce mari…d'une naissance obscure' au-dessus même du commun de la bonne bourgeoise.*" *Le Désordre des familles: Lettres de cachet des Archives de la Bastille au XVIII*[e] *siècle* (Paris: Gallimard, 2014), 194.

26 "*Ils ne fait séquestrer des filles et des icelles épousent ou fait épouser contre le gré ou vouloir des pères, mères, et parents…chose digne de punition exemplaire.*" Claude Quétel, *Une légende noire: les lettres de cachet* (Paris: Perrin, 2011), 17.

27 Claude Quétel, in *Une légende noire: les lettres de cachet* (Paris: Perrin, 2011), 17. Futher discusses this issue.
In fact, once consigned a woman could receive a *lettre de cachet* exiling them from the convent (as in the case of Geneviève de Gravelle). This action was not illegal in the 1760s and subsequently became the epitome of the arbitrary nature of power in the Old Regime, linked to Jansenist controversy. Male superiors repeatedly exiled recalcitrant nuns using the *lettres de cachet.*

28 "*La nécessité de payer une pension exclut les familles les plus humbles. Les motifs suivent et se ressemblent d'une génération à l'autre.*" Farge and Foucault, *Le Désordre des familles*, 201.

29 Among these are some of the most popular novels of the century; *La Religieuse* by Diderot, *Les Liaisons Dangereuses* by Choderlos Laclos, and *Les Lettres d'une Péruvienne* by Françoise de Graffigny are but a few.

30 Mita Choudhury, *Convents and Nuns in Eighteenth-Century French Politics and Culture* (Cornell University Press, 2004), 11-12.

31 Many women found comfort an institution that saved them from violent homes and marriages, and served as educational facilities. While Jansenists and Catholics attacked each other, the *philosophes* questioned the very premise of convents and monasteries.

32 Karen Sullivan, "Room to Grow: The Convent in Graffigny, Riccoboni, and Gouges," *The French Review* 89, no. 3 (2016): 1-2.

33 The forced vows scenario was a prevalent motif in eighteenth-century fiction about convents, especially amongst women writers. Olympe de Gouges would follow this trend with a piece on the convent for the theater.

34 "*Enfin on peut remarquer que la famille demander la lettre de cachet n'est pas noble ou tout à fait de bonne bourgeoise. Il suffit que la famille*

soit honorable, qu'aucun de ses membres ait eu à subir condamnation, d'une manière plus générale, que sa réputation soit intacte." Farge and Foucault, *Le Désordre des familles*, 201.

35 Statistically, the highest volume of letters comes from the 1740s to 1779. Farge and Foucault signal a significant downturn in the volume of letters in the years 1779-83. "*La lettre de cachet n'est pas une condamnation mais une correction, subordonnant la sortie à un amendement et l'occurrence à une conversion.*" Ibid., 191.

36 "*Le père s'adresse 'au père' historique: le roi. La lettre intégrée à la mentalité du français moyen.*" Ibid., 201.

37 Farge and Foucault see the *lettres* as a way for parents to protect their families from indiscretions. "*Femmes sur le point d'être déshonorées.*" Ibid., 9.

38 Farge and Foucault define the *lettres de cachet*: "*Le bon plaisir (du roi) royal servant à enfermer nobles infidèles ou grand vassaux des obligeants.*" Ibid., 9.

39 Vanderheyden discusses the *lettres de cachet*, pointing out that historically they constituted an indictment handed down by the king rather than an epistolary or dialogic request. *Moral Cupidity*, 1-4.

40 For further details, see Jennifer Vanderheyden, *Moral Cupidity and the Lettres de Cachet in Diderot's Writing* (Routledge, 2019), 1-5.

41 Farge and Foucault speak of how the *lettres de cachet* worked as an alternative form of justice that representented the power and mercy of the king as the "father" of the nation. Originally, it was the father who would write the request for a *placet*: "*C'est le père qui dresse la demande. Ça peut être une faute viendrait jeter le déshonneur sur une famille.*" Ibid., 206.

42 Claude Quétel in *Une légende noire*, comments on the proliferation of the *lettres* in the mid-seventeenth century, saying that the most important use of the *lettre* was working against Jansenism and the activation of *la Fronde*: "*La Fronde contribue à la prolifération des lettres de cachet.*" 192. In a similar way, Louis XV used the *lettres de cachet* to work against the proliferation of Jews in Paris. In addition, Quétel shows how the *lettres* were used in perpetuity to condemn members of the court. He recounts that Louis XVI used the power of the *lettres de cachet* later in the eighteenth century; only two days after Louis XV's death, Du Barry (*la favorite*) received a *lettre de cachet*. "*Deux jours après la mort de Louis XV, Du Barry reçoit une lettre de cachet.*" 194.

43 This research originally focused on volumes of manuscripts that included responses to the *lettres de cachet*, including the notations and documents of the police chiefs, responses from mothers superior, nuns, family members, and parents. In this study I began with a broad sweep and went through several files from 1729-1756, looking

for the responses women gave to accusations from parents, the king, husbands, landlords, and others who had been disgruntled and chosen legal recourse.

44 See Lisa Jane Graham, "Fiction, Kingship and the Politics of Character in Eighteenth-Century France," in *Mystifying the Monarch: Studies on Discourse, Power, and History*, eds. Jeroen Deploige and Gita Deneckere (Amsterdam: Amsterdam University Press, 2006): 139-58.

45 Ibid., 192.

46 Ibid.

47 "*La lettre de cachet une fois obtenue peut ne pas être mise à l'exécution, et agit alors comme une arme de dissuasion…elle fait partie de la souplesse de l'institution.*" Farge and Foucault, *Le Désordre des familles*, 207.

48 Wingrove, "Sovereign Address," 141.

49 See "Mademoiselle Bonafon and the Private Life of Louis XV: Communication Circuits in Eighteenth-Century France," *Représentations* 87, no. 1 (2004): 102-124.

50 Sarah Maza, *Private Lives and Public Affairs: The Causes Célèbres of Prerevolutionary France* (Berkeley: University of Califomia Press, 1993), 313.

51 "Victorious Victims," in *Going Public: Women and Publishing in Early Modern Times,* eds. Elizabeth Goldsmith and Dena Goodman (Ithaca: Cornell University Press, 1995), 62-78.

52 "Often the lawyers would represent women especially nuns as monsters and as subject of Aristocratic depravity." Ibid., 63.

53 *Cachet* is the word for the red wax seal on the letter, announcing the authority of the king.

54 Wingrove, "Sovereign Address," 139.

55 Ibid.

56 See Goodman, *Becoming a Woman*, and this apt summation of her work from Aurora Wolfgang: "Thus, while focusing on the private practice of women's letter writing, Goodman elucidates the many ways in which this practice embedded women within social networks of family and friends, the larger modern world at home and abroad, and ultimately the movements of Enlightenment France." "Review of *Becoming a Woman in the Age of Letters*, by Dena Goodman," *Eighteenth-Century Studies* 48, no. 4 (2015): 546-547.

References

Abrams, Barbara. "Decoding Hospitality: Image and Polity in Rousseau's *Lévite d'Ephraïm*." In *Reframing Rousseau's Lévite D'Ephraïm: The Hebrew Bible, Hospitality, and Modern Identity*, 90–124. Liverpool University Press, 2021.

Badinter, Élisabeth. *Émilie, Émilie: L'ambition féminine au 18ième siècle*. Paris: Flammarion, 1983.

Berenguier, Nadine. "Victorious Victims." In *Going Public: Women and Publishing in Early Modern Times*, edited by Elizabeth Goldsmith and Dena Goodman, 62–78. Ithaca: Cornell University Press, 1995.

Choudhury, Mita. *Convents and Nuns in Eighteenth-Century French Politics and Culture*. Cornell University Press, 2004.

Darnton, Robert. "Mademoiselle Bonafon and the Private Life of Louis XV: Communication Circuits in Eighteenth-Century France." *Représentations* 87, no. 1 (2004): 102–124.

Farge, Arlette and Michel Foucault. *Le Désordre des familles: Lettres de cachet des Archives de la Bastille au XVIIIe siècle*. Paris: Gallimard, 2014.

Goodman, Dena. *Becoming a Women in the Age of Letters*. Ithaca: Cornell University Press, 2009.

Goodman, Dena. *The Republic of Letters: A Cultural History of the French Enlightenment*. Ithaca: Cornell University Press, 1994.

Goodman, Dena. "Enlightenment Salons: The Convergence of Female and Philosophic Ambitions." *Eighteenth-Century Studies* 22, no. 3 (1989): 329–50.

Graham, Lisa Jane. "Fiction, Kingship and the Politics of Character in Eighteenth-Century France." In *Mystifying the Monarch: Studies on Discourse, Power, and History*, edited by Jeroen Deploige and Gita Deneckere, 139–58. Amsterdam: Amsterdam University Press, 2006.

Landes, Joan. *Women and the Public Sphere in the Age of the French Revolution*. Ithaca: Cornell University Press, 1988.

MacArthur, Elizabeth J. "Devious Narratives: Refusal of Closure in Two Eighteenth-Century Epistolary Novels." *Eighteenth-Century Studies* 21, no. 1 (1987): 1–20.

Maza, Sarah. *Private Lives and Public Affairs: The Causes Célèbres* of *Prerevolutionary France*. Berkeley: University of Califomia Press, 1993.

McDonald, Christie. "Mapping the Strategies for the 18th Century Section of *Femmes, littérature. Une histoire culturelle* (in progress): *libertés, égalités, dilemmes*." Lecture at the Mahindra Humanities Center, Harvard University, 1 February 2017. https://complit.fas.harvard.edu/event/mapping-strategies-18th-century-section-femmes-littérature-une-histoire-culturelle

Quétel, Claude. *Une légende noire: les lettres de cachet*. Paris: Perrin, 2011.

Rancière, Jacques. *The Politics of Aesthetics: The Distribution of the Sensible*. Translated by Gabriel Rockhill. London: Continuum, 2006.

Rancière, Jacques. *The Names of History: On the Poetics of Knowledge*. Translated by Hassan Melehy. Minneapolis: University of Minnesota Press, 1994.

Rousseau, Jean-Jacques. *Émile*. In *Oeuvres Complètes*. Vol. 4, *Émile–Éducation–Morale–Botanique*. Edited by Bernard Gagnebin and Marcel Raymond. Paris: Bibliothèque de la Pléiade, Gallimard, 1969

Rousseau, Jean-Jacques. *Politics and the Arts: Letter to D'Alembert on the Theatre*. Edited and translated by Alan Bloom. Ithaca: Cornell University Press, 1964.

Rousseau, Jean-Jacques. *La Nouvelle Héloïse*. In *Oeuvres Complètes*. Vol. 2, *La Nouvelle Héloïse–Théâtre–Poésies–Essais littéraires*. Edited by Bernard Gagnebin and Marcel Raymond. Paris: Bibliothèque de la Pléiade, Gallimard, 1961.

Rousseau, Jean-Jacques. *Les Confessions*. In *Oeuvres Complètes*. Vol. 1, *Les Confessions–Autres textes autobiographiques*. Edited by Bernard Gagnebin and Marcel Raymond. Paris: Bibliothèque de la Pléiade, Gallimard, 1959.

Sullivan, Karen. "Room to Grow: The Convent in Graffigny, Riccoboni, and Gouges." *The French Review* 89, no. 3 (2016): 161–74.

Vanderheydan, Jennifer. *Moral Cupidity and the Lettres de Cachet in Diderot's Writing*. Routledge, 2019.

Wingrove, Elizabeth. "Sovereign Address." *Political Theory* 40, no. 2 (2012): 135–164.

Wolfgang, Aurora. Review of *Becoming a Woman in the Age of Letters*, by Dena Goodman. *Eighteenth-Century Studies* 48, no. 4 (2015): 546–547.

2 *Les Causes Célèbres*, Factum or Fiction? or: "That's What He Said!"

In mid-eighteenth-century France, literary publications begin to focus on the activity of the courtroom, as the more current-events-oriented stories lend individuals a collective sense of purpose by appealing to their great appetites and the reading public's desire for sensationalist accounts. Many writers, including the *philosophes,* turned their focus to tragic cases and popular accounts of misconduct. Voltaire played a major role in this shift in 1770, when he brought the Calas affair to the attention of the public by way of his passionate appeal and detailed description of the case.[1] The eighteenth-century public had an avid interest in reading about specific cases, brought mainly against women, for all types of malfeasance and behavioral infractions. As more women were relegated to convents, workhouses, and prisons, their stories were fictionalized and expanded in various print forms and literature. In eighteenth-century France, the more well-known examples of these types of public scandal cases include works such as Diderot's *La Religieuse*, the epistolary novel that draws upon and fictionalizes the real-life experience of Marguerite Delamarre.[2]

Robert Darnton has argued that both the problem and the solution to the questions of the ideological and cultural origins of the French Revolution could be revealed in an examination of the literary world.[3] In response to Darnton's challenge, Sarah Maza in *Private Lives and Public Affairs, The Causes Célèbres of Prerevolutionary France* introduces her thesis with these words: "This book is about stories, about the public impact of tales of private life."[4] The discussion that follows here explores the

DOI: 10.4324/9780429001147-3

literary nature of some of these tales of private life in eighteenth-century France, and specifically underscores how they are turned from historical testimony or evidence into fictional literature. In addition, I suggest a new tack so that we may expand our understanding of these "tales." By centering the discussion on the literary value of this work, we may gain insight into the literary production narrating the lives of sequestered and aggrieved women and assess how it contributes to our understanding of history. Indeed, we may appreciate the evolution of literary style as a reflection of history rather than as mere raw material, or as a rough draft of historiography.

The following questions may help establish this process of literary examination:

1. How does the evolution of literature and knowledge of the literary process bring light to historical truth?
2. What were the *mémoires judiciaires*?
3. How does the concept of the role of gender play a significant part in the evolution of our understanding of what was constructed as literary in the eighteenth century and how is that different today?
4. How does legal literature derived from the *mémoires judiciaires* prove to be problematic and even dangerous when fictionalized?

We often look at history to help us define what literature is today.[5] Yet, when one considers the history of literature and its definition, we come up with a troubling set of problematics, often because of the modern standards and theories we have come to impose upon our interpretations of literary production. Many of the ways we categorize writing do not lend themselves to an adequate or complete definition of a genre, nor are the forms of writing a good fit for a particular "ism" or definition. So often we try to modify, modernize, and develop these categories. Our understanding of early modern Western literature is defined by a confluence of historical, sociological, and literary-critical perspectives, which apply more broadly to the eighteenth century. With newer modes of reading, we can keep defining literary studies by considering the actual product in its authentic contexts. The authenticity of such readings helps us further understand historiography.

The evolution of Western European literature, and specifically the mid-seventeenth century in France, owes much to the court of Louis XIV. Under his reign, he standardized language and formed an academy that would eventually influence and define the genres of "literature" for centuries to come. France was unlike any other country in Europe during the seventeenth century in that the king was an absolute monarch, holding sway over matters of the church. In contrast, other Catholic countries followed the papal orders and rulings that dictated matters of the church. The French church and state had little or no separation, and the king had the right to rule on all matters of religious law and jurisprudence. In theory, the political power of the king derived from the Renaissance idea that a ruler should inspire obedience through exemplary behavior and affection rather than by force, as he was the embodiment of God and reason.

The relationship between politics, the law, and literature acquired unprecedented force during the reign of Louis XIV. The monarchical system of governance persisted long into the eighteenth century and did not provide a mechanism for separation of church and state. Matters of law were under the aegis of the king as well, even though, in practice, there were many matters of law that did not involve the king.[6] The matters of justice were handled by the police chief and the police. The police chief was court appointed and wielded a great deal of power.

As the epistolary novel was gaining popularity, letters, judicial *mémoires*, and factums increasingly served as a seemingly endless source of material for literature that represented real events in people's lives. At this time, legal documents recorded by the court, lawyers, or scribes were called the *mémoires judiciaires* or the factum. On the one hand, the legal brief became its own form of scandal literature and, on the other hand, replies and responses to the briefs also helped to set the stage for a consideration of a new form of literature. The factum material helps us understand the real testimony of the people who were the subjects of the *mémoires judiciaires*, the *Causes Célèbres* and other forms of legal briefs.

Lawyers in the second half of the eighteenth century use sensational courtroom documents and begin to shape them into a new form of literary rhetoric (that eventually eclipses the real story).[7] Thus the *Causes Célèbres* are stories told by men (lawyers) and though some vignettes are focused on men, there is a surprising emphasis on cases representing women. The authors take evidentiary information and embellish, hyperbolize, and, often advertise facts that in turn advance both public and literary agendas. The popularized stories based on actual legal cases were not unlike today's popular *Law and Order* TV series, which always claims to be "ripped from the headlines." Sarah Maza examines the collection of legal briefs, describes the *mémoires judiciaires*, and explains in great detail how this legal work was transformed into a literary work titled *Causes Célèbres*. This combined legal and literary effort became a commercialized and lucrative response to the public's insatiable demand for reports of scandal. Maza and Darnton both look upon these briefs as historical evidence and forms of the "endless possibilities of print medium."[8] In this exploration, we further the process of investigation by looking at the literary content and context of these documents to help inform us of the historical import.

The approach of reading forensic literature and using objects to support our further understanding points to what Nancy Miller so often referred to as the "gendering" of storytelling and less often to the "fictionalizing" of literature.[9] Seeing the stories through the lens of gender helps us consider that the lawyers who were the authors of these legal briefs sought to objectify the experiences of people suffering to pander to the hunger of the scandal-seeking crowds. The topics of these briefs were predominantly stories about women and their painful experiences. These briefs included the full content of the legal file. The analysis that follows will explain how the material objects and the literature in the file were used as a mechanism of exploitation. The women's stories were sensationalized in order to create a good story and increase its lucrative value for writers and publishers, while the original texts authored by many women still go largely ignored.[10]

Much of what we term today simply as *mémoires* and other materials relevant to the case are embedded and lumped together with the legal documents that are maintained for archival purposes. In her work on the *Causes Célèbres*, Maza has established that the factum and *mémoires judiciaires* are one and the same, and I would propose a further refinement of these terms. Many *mémoires judiciaires* files are in the Arsenal Library and more specifically the Archives de la Bastille. The individual dossiers include a collection of materials that contain much more than the narrative from the lawyers, and the sum total of the documents confirm the notion that they are hybrid texts. The documents of a case file include diverse content: personal notes and letters to family, lists of groceries and sundries that the plaintiff or sometimes the prisoner needed—even forms and memorabilia.[11]

The legal briefs, which were part of the *mémoires judiciaires*, were signed by the lawyer for the client and then were often published for public consumption. It seems that these were legal documents, though lawyers were free from the obligation to seek royal approval.[12] The whole brief/file is a synthesis between literary forms, objects, letters, lists, and juridical language. It is clear that both the *mémoires* and the factum generated other forms of literature and inspired authors (such as Voltaire and Diderot).

Factum and *Mémoire*: The Role of Letters and Evidence

What is the relationship between the judicial memoir, the factum, and the letters, citations, accounts, or *mémoires*? All these written expressions were interwoven and interrelated in the context of eighteenth-century France. All of these written pieces found their way into the legal brief. Jean Sgard and Hans-Jürgen Lüsebrink have estimated that there were nine collections, 23 editions, and 253 volumes published between these years. Sgard and Lüsebrink highlight the fact that the language of the law borrowed from the language of emotions and that the lawyers popularized the briefs to disseminate them to satisfy public interest.[13]

The *Causes Célèbres* was a subscription collection that was motivated by the public's desire to read the *mémoires judiciaires.* Often, these testimonies were appropriated by lawyers, and in particular by Nicolas-Toussaint le Moyne des Essarts, notably in his 1773 *Causes Célèbres, curieuses et intéressantes, de toutes les cours souveraines du royaume, avec les jugements qui les ont décidées.* Des Essarts' compilations of the files in the *Causes Célèbres* were very popular between 1734 and 1789. In the "*XVII*[e] *CAUSE*" of volume three of the *Causes Célèbres*, all cases pertained to the topic of "*Adultere*" (adultery).[14] Here the lawyer Des Essarts used the cases brought before a judge as fodder for public judgment and to fuel the misogyny of eighteenth-century French society. The added pressures of propaganda and censorship create tensions but produce rich literature.

As we probe deeper into this material, we acquire a better understanding of the evolution of what literature comprises, especially when the academy seeks to apply its own traditional tools of analysis. We must keep questioning both the tradition and its tools. It is helpful to view the entire brief, including documents written by lawyers and those left by the individual defendants, as a unified set. This approach helps us differentiate the forms of writing that were converging at the time. The factum with all its contents is, as Sarah Maza underscored, a hybrid form of legal language and literary rhetoric, and the non-legal letters preserve the handwritten testimony, or authentic voice of the person accused of the crime. Thus, considering the whole of the file of *mémoires judiciaires* lends a fuller picture of the "affair." In addition to the materials already mentioned by Maza and in this article, the file could include not only personalized *mémoires*, letters to and from family members, priests, mothers superior, and others—it is the whole record of the accused women, leading to their incarceration and from the time of their consignment.

The factum/*mémoires judiciaires* is a form of writ or legal document. The French term *mémoires judiciaires* is often used interchangeably (and confusingly) with the word factum. The narrative part of the document was referred to as "*faits*" (facts) and the legal argument was called the "*moyens*" (means).

In the eighteenth century, there were a number of published *mémoires* and printed factums, or legal briefs. I would like to emphasize that lawyers summarized the intention of the judges, the causes, the facts, and the orders/demands of a particular legal procedure. They were more or less detailed documents, depending on the case and the social status of the plaintiffs whom they represented. The length would often depend on the importance of the case and could range anywhere from two to 500 pages. In the case of high or middle nobility, the king himself may have read the factum, thus underscoring a certain attention to the heightened level and formulaic language of the legal part of the brief. The women's accounts were told in a very straightforward manner. Sometimes the testimonies were written down by the scribe or the lawyer. Later on, these inclusions in the *Causes Célèbres* lent an impression of seriousness to the "telling of the story."[15]

Figure 2.1 Documents from legal (*prisonner*) files found in the Archives de la Bastille, which include pieces of fabrics and instructions for dressmaking. Photograph by the author.

Note: Documents from legal files found in Paris, Archives de la Bastille (AB), including pieces of fabrics and instructions for dressmaking. MS 11785, 317.

The legal brief was often written by a scribe and then edited and composed by a lawyer. The clergy or the police could offer documents to add to the case. Robert Darnton emphasizes that the spread of the message and how it reached the public and took hold mattered more than its origin in sociocultural terms. All cases were not included in the *Causes Célèbres* but by means of gossip and word of mouth, all cases eventually made their way to the public circles.

The factum is, in large part, the testimony, and, especially in the cases of women's adultery, the husband related his version to the lawyer. It is factum that seals the male voice of the case. As Geraldine Ther says: "The husband is validated for the most part in the factum."[16] While the legal brief is a very important part of the collection that makes up the factum, women also actually told their stories and wrote or dictated their versions of the tale. The more personalized writings by women are in the form of letters, and often there is a diary (a sort of *mémoire*) accompanying the factum in the case files. What remains clear through the eighteenth century up to the twenty-first is that the factum remained a masculinist form of expression, and it could also be embellished. Thus, fiction influenced the outcome of the case as well.[17]

Ther separates and defines the different forms of factums. She explains that the factums are a global reflection of how women were presented by male authority, especially in the *mémoires judiciaires*. Many of the included materials—diaries, letters, and *mémoires*—were reports about women by women. The legal brief section of the factum was a report made by men, and obviously this communication could not help but be a stumbling block for some types of discourse, themes, and questions that the lawyers (all men) had to deal with. The lawyers would choose certain examples that derived from jurisprudence in order to evoke scandal and/or public sympathy.[18] Ther poses the following question when speaking of the function of the factums vis-à-vis their role in governance and society: "In what capacity were the factums helpful in proving that women could occupy a first place rank in society, even though they often diffused stereotyped speech?"[19] A partial answer to Ther's question would be to regard the factum as a snapshot of the disempowerment of women in this context.

Case Studies within the *Causes Célèbres*

Within the case studies of *Causes Célèbres*, one case stands out as an example of the type of public and literary abuse that was perpetrated by lawyers. This case is discussed in detail by Nadine Berenguier in "Victorious Victims." In her analysis, Berenguier assesses the case of Gabrielle-Geneviève Fargès and, Louis-Jacques Boudin, and the lover, Nicholas Bruchon.

In this case, Maître Simon Nicholas Linguet, the popular lawyer from the famous Calas affair, submitted a file, that of Mme Boudin, who was mostly a constructed character, a theory to be defended in an interesting jurisprudence case.[20] Linguet used true cases as material to produce his own literature. In his prolific writings about these cases, Linguet embellished real trial stories that glorified women's suffering. At the end of the Boudin case, the lady was released from the convent after a time, but she was still vilified and victimized by the media as a result of the notoriety she had received. All Parisians were aware of her infidelity. Yet she was but a construct: *un personnage féminin à défendre*, or: feminine character to protect, according to Nadine Berenguier.[21]

Popular Case Studies

Another popular case in eighteenth-century France involves Mlle de Nogent. It was most recently analyzed by Jennifer Vanderheyden in 2014. She finds that the narrative strategies of familiar complaints escalate to a dangerous level, and consequentially the reader is implicated in a critical epistemology that ultimately requires drawing personal conclusions regarding culpability.[22]

In much of his work, Robert Darnton moves from questions of production to those of circulation and access to clandestine literature. He examines rhetoric that was not intended as literature at the time, including many forms of discourse encompassing oral and print media. In another well-known case, that of Mlle Bonafon, Darnton uses an archival case file. His study of Bonafon involves the chambermaid-author who was sent to a convent because of her portrayal of the court in her theatrical piece called *Tanastès*. Darnton says that Bonafon transmitted the mythical nature and the folklore of the court; he also estimates that the king deemed her play capable of undermining the French court.[23] This

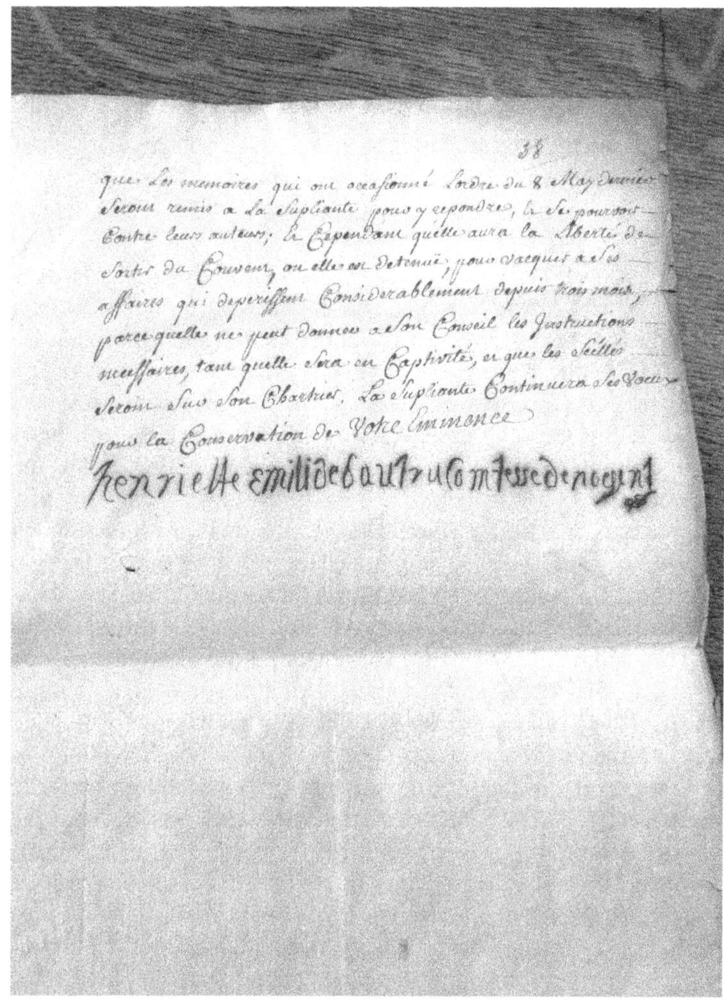

38

que les memoires qui ont occasionné l'ordre du 8 May dernier
seront remis a la Supliante pour y repondre, et se pourvoir
contre leurs auteurs; et cependant qu'elle aura la liberté de
sortir du Couvent, ou elle est detenuë, pour vacquer a ses
affaires qui deperissent considerablement depuis trois mois,
parce qu'elle ne peut donner a son Conseil les instructions
necessaires, tant qu'elle sera en captivité, et que les scellés
seront sur son chartier. La Supliante continuera ses voeux
pour la conservation de votre Eminence

henriette emillie de bautru comtesse de nogent

Figure 2.2 Example of page with signature of consignee, Henriette Émilie de Nogent. Photograph by the author.

Source: AB, MS 11504, 38.

case became immensely popular, not by way of its connection to the literary quality of the play—indeed quite the opposite. It was sensationalized by the documents surrounding the case and the dissemination of gossip in the public sphere.[24] Lisa Jane Graham has commented upon this phenomenon: "Many directed this attention towards the crown, others experimented with new genres such as the novel, that enabled self-expression and criticism." Graham argues that form plays a determining role in this type of literature.[25]

The case of Mme Gravelle was not well known until Jacques Rancière's work in 1992, which treated letters authored by women in challenging circumstances as political testimony. Later in 2012, Elizabeth Wingrove treats this idea as an enticement to use and interpret certain letters. She does argue that literature is indeed a strong tool in the forensic study of history. She does not, however, look into the *mémoires judiciares* as a whole, but selects the Gravelle file as a particular case study, and even then, she only transcribes a portion of the file.[26] The reasons for this approach become obvious when handing over the file. It is over 260 pages long, and it includes many rambling and unintelligible letters and replies, including lists and orders placed by Gravelle herself.

This said, it may well be that the later, more unraveled part of Gravelle's file is the most important for this study, if we choose to "read" the objects of this file. We see the disarray of her life through the very chaotic nature of her expression. Her writing is both a literary and political tool. The act of reading about the objects, as well as the notes, lists, and the order forms fills out the narrative. This approach offers a richly expanded set of resources and readings as theorists and historians continue to consider women's agency in eighteenth-century France. In the most illegible parts of the manuscript, Gravelle herself confesses: "Perhaps you'll have trouble reading these [text indecipherable] details…as I've hardly the leisure to finish or think my words, in such a situation, one must write voluminously."[27] Gravelle's claims to political standing are exploited and, at this point, the literary becomes political. This is of course a vexing issue, and one must reconsider the question: is the *mémoire* itself canonical?[28]

The consideration of the *mémoires judiciaires* as a forensic literary context is key to addressing this question. Regarding the information we gather from the entire brief, an authentic piece

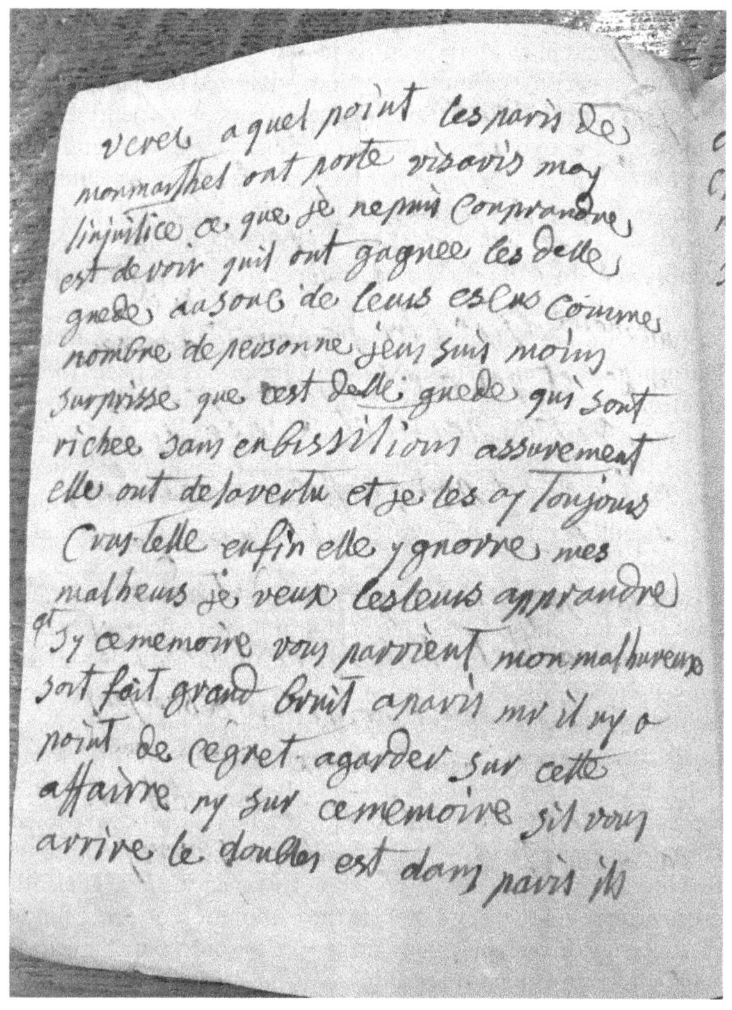

verel a quel point les paris de
monmarthel ont porte visavis moy
linjustice ce que je nepuis Comprandre
est de voir quil ont gagnee les delle
guede aasone de leurs escus comme
nombre de personne jeen suis moins
surprisse que cest delle guede qui sont
richee sans enbissitions assurement
elle ont de la vertu et je les ay Toujours
Cruy telle enfin elle ygnorre mes
malheurs je veux lesleurs apprandre
et sy cememoire vous parvient mon malheureux
sort fait grand bruit aparis mr il ny a
point de regret agarder sur cette
affairre ny sur cememoire sil vous
arrive le doubler est dans paris ils

Figure 2.3 Example of the chaotic nature of Gravelle's expression, as evidenced by her handwriting. Photograph by the author.

Source: AB, MS 11769, 118.

of history, it provides powerful forensic tools to contextualize the recorded events. It does not mean that what is recounted in the brief is factual in every respect. As in any situation, we well know how stories become permutated by individualized perspectives and embellishments over time. Reading the entirety of a brief does add dimensionality to our initial understanding of the culture and context of the time. In assessing the literary value of these documents, it proves to be a very important tool, both in terms of what the forensic testimony offers us today and in light of how we begin records and stories in early modern times to suit the needs of the reading (and listening) public.

Today we are living in an era characterized by what Robert Darnton has termed "literary opportunism" as applied to the eighteenth century—especially in regard to fictionalizing women's stories to expose them to an eager public. The early modern era is the most literary. In fact, an immense quantity of "literature" had been produced.[29] Much of the evidence located within the documents pertaining to the *mémoires judiciaires* remains overlooked.

In the discussion of the literary nature of these stories (and their metamorphosis from historical testimony to fictitious storytelling), we must also be aware that they are documents that set the stage for a consideration of a new form of literature also authored by the people who were the subjects of the *Causes Célèbres* and other forms of legal briefs. We must remain alert to the reality that, in some respects, even the legal factums are false, in that they represent a form of storytelling; they are a literary product rooted in real-life experience. A completer and more focused picture of this literature and history, especially of women in the eighteenth century, may emerge if we include the exploration of other forms of literature that supplement these stories and contribute to a fuller understanding of the truth.

Notes

1 See W. D. Howarth, "Tragedy into Melodrama: The Fortunes of the Calas Affair on Stage," *Studies on Voltaire and the Eighteenth Century* 174 (1978): 125–126.

2 Georges May, *Diderot et "La Religieuse": Étude Historique et Littéraire* (New Haven: Yale University Press, 1954).

3 "In Search of Enlightenment: Recent Attempts to Create a Social History of Ideas," *Journal of Modern History* 43 (March 1971): 113–132.

4 *Private Lives and Public Affairs, The Causes Célèbres of Prerevolutionary France* (Berkeley: University of California Press: 1993), 1.

5 Stephan Greenblatt for one promotes the ideas of "new historicism" as a helpful way to read literature. See Sarah Maza's commentary on Greenblatt's literary commentaries in "Stephen Greenblatt, New Historicism, and Cultural History, or, What We Talk About When We Talk About Interdisciplinarity," *Modern Intellectual History* 1, no. 2 (2004): 249–65.

6 There was one mechanism reserved for the king that had greater power than that of the police and superseded jurisprudence. The *lettres de cachet* were above the authority of the courts and subject to no other appeal than that of the king's benevolence in censorship of his own judgment. By their very nature there is a question of their function with respect to jurisprudence and the rhetoric of the court. For further insight see Arlette Farge and Michel Foucault. Their discussion focuses specifically on the use of the letters by the aristocracy. "*Mirabeau a contesté les lettres à toute puissance du (sovereign) souverain mise à la disposition du public.*" *Le Désordre des familles: Lettres de cachet des Archives de la Bastille au XVIIIe siècle* (Paris: Gallimard, 2014), 430.

7 "By the later 1770s trial briefs gave unprecedented publicity to the scandalous underside of upper-class life, while the employment of a successful brief frequently included a debunking of aristocratic morgue and power. Thanks to court cases and *mémoires* the private theatre of upper-class life had been forced open: *le public* was well on its way to becoming *l'opinion publique.*" Maza, *Causes Célèbres,* 166.

8 See ibid., 115.

9 Nancy Miller, *The Poetics of Gender* (New York: Columbia University Press: 1986), 270.

10 "In litigations pitting women against male relatives, however, publicity was always a strategy that carried special risks. In such cases women were breaking the mold of ideal womanhood shaped by much of the moral and pedagogical literature of the period which prescribed modesty, acceptance of a life led in obscurity, submission, and self-control as the most acceptable forms of female behavior." Nadine Berenguier, "Victorious Victims," in *Going Public: Women and Publishing in Early Modern Times* eds. Elizabeth Goldsmith and Dena Goodman (Ithaca: Cornell University Press, 1995), 63.

11 "The lawyers' role took place essentially outside the courtroom and consisted mainly in the drafting of yet another set of documents, which they presented to the judges on their client's behalf. A lawyer's brief, could range in length from a few pages to several hundred,

traditionally comprised first a narration of the case from his client's point of view (*les faits*) and then the technical discussion (*les moyens*). These documents were called factums, or more commonly referred to as *mémoires*—a term that means memorandum, but that had suggestive historical or autobiographical connotations. *Mémoires* were originally handwritten and were theoretically destined solely for use within the courtroom, where they were read aloud to or consulted by the judges before the final verdict. Over the course of the seventh century, however the custom had developed of printing such documents in multiple copies so that friends, relatives, and other interested parties could be apprised of the lines along which the case was being argued, and of its progress." Maza, *Causes Célèbres,* 35.

12 "To the modern reader, two features of this procedure, which applied in both lower courts and the courts of appeal, will seem especially remarkable: first, the process took place entirely in private, behind closed doors; and the second, although plaintiff and defendant could seek aid from lawyers, they usually faced the judge alone, in the absence of their counsel." Ibid., 34–5.

13 Hans-Jürgen Lüsebrink, "L'affaire Cléreaux (Rouen, 1786): affrontement idéologique et tensions institutionelles autour de la scène judiciare au XVIIIe siècle," *Studies on Voltaire and the Eighteenth Century* 191 (1980): 894–900 and Jean Sgard, "La littérature des *Causes Célèbres*," in *Approches des Lumière. Mélanges offerts à Jean Fabre* (Paris: Klincksieck, 1974), 459–70.

14 Nicolas-Toussaint le Moyne des Essarts, *Causes célèbres, curieuses et intéressantes, de toutes les cours souveraines du royaume, avec les jugemens qui les ont décidées*, vol. 3 (Paris: 1773), 116, https://gallica.bnf.fr/ark:/12148/bpt6k92335s.

15 "To be sure the incendiary *remonstrances* of the eighteenth-century courts were often banned and published legally." Maza, *Causes Célèbres*, 5.

16 "*Le mari est valorisé pour la plupart dans des factums.*" *Jeux de rôles et de Pouvoirs. La représentation des femmes (1770–1789)* (Dijon: Éditions Universitaires de Dijon, collection *Histoires*, 2017), 45.

17 Ibid., 45–46.

18 Ibid., 45.

19 "*Dans quelle mesure les factums, alors qu'ils diffusent des discours stéréotypés, peuvent-ils admettre que les femmes puissent occuper une place de premier plan dans la société*?" Ibid., 16.

20 *Précis pour Gabrielle-Geneviève Fargès, épouse du sieur Boudin, et par l'accusée d'adultère* (Paris: 1773), https://gallica.bnf.fr/ark:/12148/bpt6k72340z.

21 "*D'une façon il construit une image d'une bourgeoise dévouée. Mme Boudin a inondé le public de ses mémoires.*" Boudin's reasoning

according to her letters is to *"conserver son image et sa réputation juridique.*" Berenguier, "Victorious Victims," 135.
22 *Moral Cupidity and the Lettres de Cachet in Diderot's Writing* (New York: Routledge, 2019).
23 Robert Darnton, "Mademoiselle Bonafon and the Private Life of Louis XV: Communication Circuits in Eighteenth-Century France," *Representations* 87, no. 1 (2004): 102–124.
24 Ibid.
25 Lisa Jane Graham, "Fiction, Kingship and the Politics of Character in Eighteenth-Century France," in *Mystifying the Monarch: Studies on Discourse, Power and History*, eds. Jeroen Deploige and Gita Deneckere (Amsterdam: Amsterdam University Press, 2006), 139–158.
26 See Elizabeth Wingrove's discussion of Rancière's work in "Sovereign Address," *Political Theory* 40, no. 2 (2012): 135–64.
27 Ibid.
28 See "Sovereign Power," where Wingrove begins the set-up for the consideration of what is political and what is literary in Gravelle's case file.
29 Historians and literary scholars, including Dena Goodman, Elizabeth Goldsmith, Sarah Maza, Robert Darnton, Roger Chartier, Stephan Greenblatt, Elizabeth Wingrove, and many others, have documented much of this evidence in recent decades.

References

Berenguier, Nadine. "Victorious Victims." In *Going Public: Women and Publishing in Early Modern Times,* edited by Elizabeth Goldsmith and Dena Goodman, 62–78. Ithaca: Cornell University Press, 1995.

Darnton, Robert. "Mademoiselle Bonafon and the Private Life of Louis XV: Communication Circuits in Eighteenth-Century France." *Representations* 87, no. 1 (2004): 102–24.

Darnton, Robert. "In Search of the Enlightenment: Recent Attempts to Create a Social History of Ideas." *The Journal of Modern History* 43, no. 1 (1971): 113–32.

Des Essarts, Nicolas-Toussaint le Moyne. *Causes célèbres, curieuses et intéressantes, de toutes les cours souveraines du royaume, avec les jugemens qui les ont décidées*. Vol. 3. Paris: Archives de la Bastille, 1773. https://gallica.bnf.fr/ark:/12148/bpt6k92335s.

Farge, Arlette and Michel Foucault. *Le Désordre des familles: Lettres de cachet des Archives de la Bastille au XVIIIe siècle*. Paris: Gallimard, 2014.

Goodman, Dena. *The Republic of Letters: A Cultural History of the French Enlightenment*. Ithaca: Cornell University Press, 1994.

Graham, Lisa Jane. "Fiction, Kingship and the Politics of Character in Eighteenth-Century France." In *Mystifying the Monarch: Studies on Discourse, Power and History*, edited by Jeroen Deploige and Gita Deneckere, 139–158. Amsterdam: Amsterdam University Press, 2006.

Howarth, W. D. "Tragedy into Melodrama: The Fortunes of the Calas Affair on Stage." *Studies on Voltaire and the Eighteenth Century* 174 (1978): 125–126.

Linguet, Simon-Nicolas-Henri. *Précis pour Gabrielle-Geneviève Fargès, épouse du sieur Boudin, et par l'accusée d'adultère.* Paris: 1773. https://gallica.bnf.fr/ark:/12148/bpt6k72340z

Lüsebrink, Hans-Jürgen. "L'affaire Cléreaux (Rouen, 1786): affrontement idéologique et tensions institutionelles autour de la scène judiciare au XVIIIe siècle." *Studies on Voltaire and the Eighteenth Century* 191 (1980): 894–900.

May, Georges. *Diderot et "La Religieuse": Étude Historique et Littéraire.* New Haven: Yale University Press, 1954.

Maza, Sarah. "Stephen Greenblatt, New Historicism, and Cultural History, or, What We Talk About When We Talk About Interdisciplinarity." *Modern Intellectual History* 1, no. 2 (2004): 249–65.

Maza, Sarah. *Private Lives and Public Affairs, The Causes Célèbres of Prerevolutionary France*. Berkeley: University of California Press, 1993.

Miller, Nancy K. *The Poetics of Gender*. New York: Columbia University Press, 1986.

Sgard, Jean. "La literature des Causes Célèbres." In *Approches des Lumières. Mélanges offerts à Jean Fabre*, 459–470. Paris: Klincksieck, 1974.

Ther, Geraldine. *Jeux de rôles et de Pouvoirs. La représentation des femmes (1770–1789)*. Dijon: Éditions Universitaires de Dijon, collection *Histoires*, 2017.

Vanderheyden, Jennifer. *Moral Cupidity and the Lettres de Cachet in Diderot's Writing*. New York: Routledge, 2017.

Wingrove, Elizabeth. "Sovereign Address." *Political Theory* 40, no. 2 (2012): 135–64.

3 *Tanastès* est Satan

Authenticity and Audacity in the Writings of Marie-Madeleine Bonafon

Epistolary Style, Oral Tradition, the Development of the Novel and Other Forms of Women's Writing in Eighteenth-Century France

In this chapter we read the letters written by a woman, Mlle Marie Bonafon, who was arrested and confined to the Bastille for writing a scandalous play about the king and his love life, titled *Tanastès*. She was later consigned to a convent since she became ill and weak in prison. Subsequently, she wrote numerous letters to the various authorities over twelve years trying to secure her own release. Outside the drama of *Tanastès*, the "roman-à-clef," there are dimensions of resistance in the letters written from inside the prison and the convent.[1] Reading and reviewing the case file of Mlle Bonafon sheds light on the importance of her place in history as a writer. It is also a central consideration of this study to treat her letter writing after she stopped writing for the public and to examine the relationship between these two types of literary production.

Much scholarship on eighteenth-century French letter writing thus far has discussed the fact that epistolary literature is rooted in correspondence and therefore linked to the oral tradition of dialogue and conversation. There has been some investigation of the epistolary style in literature of the eighteenth century by scholars of eighteenth-century France. It can be said that the eighteenth-century literary tradition traces much of its development to different writing styles. The writing of actual letters was at the center of many Enlightenment concepts: politesse, wit, reason, manners, and aesthetics were all included as part of an ethos of

DOI: 10.4324/9780429001147-4

correspondence. In fact, readers relied on correspondence as a more true and authentic kind of writing.[2] With women, this aesthetic may have seemed particularly cultivated. In the seventeenth century, women's epistolary art effectively went underground, but not in a clandestine or repressed way. It remained, so to speak, near the surface, cultivated in private homes.

In the eighteenth century, a parallel form in the development of writing technique was taking place in the genre of the novel. Readers were becoming more interested in writing and reading literature of all sorts. As stated earlier, the eighteenth century was an increasingly literary period. While the worlds of letter writing and novel writing collided with the development of the epistolary novel, letter writing in the eighteenth century remains a sub-category that is largely unexplored and proves especially interesting when asking questions surrounding women's agency, involvement in the Enlightenment, and their spheres of influence.

Bonafon and the "Affaire Bonafon"

Marie-Madeleine Bonafon was born on October 20, 1716 in Versailles, the daughter of Jean-Pierre de Bonafon, *écuyer*, or stable master, to Sieur d'Albert, and Marie Le Noir. She was sometimes referred to as Marie-Madeleine Bonafous d'Albert. She was educated at the Abbaye de Pentemont. At twenty-three years of age, she gained employment and served as *femme de chambre* to the Princesse Catherine-Eléonore de Montauban and moved to the Palace of Versailles. Bonafon's social station would have given her some opportunity to absorb at least a moderate level of literary proficiency and exposure to some of the literature of her time. Certainly, her social position gave her access to the court. In service there, Bonafon seems to have put her basic convent education to good use in writing novels and plays. While only the novel *Tanastès* is known to have survived, several others are referred to in the legal briefs.

We do not know when Bonafon's literary production at court began, but we do know for a certainty that in 1745, at the age of twenty-eight, Bonafon published her inflammatory novel *Tanastès*, about the intrigues of the court of Louis XV.[3] Claude Henri Feydeau de Marville, the lieutenant general chief of police, directed the interrogation. Bonafon was subsequently imprisoned in the Bastille for the duration of her interrogation and then relegated to a convent in 1748, where she remained unhappily for a period of twelve years. The terms of the sentence specified that Bonafon be deprived of pen and paper and disallowed visitors. Nevertheless, Bonafon was resourceful in finding ways to communicate with many people of consequence, especially the police secretary, M. Duval. Bonafon created a network of correspondents and managed a campaign to lobby for her release. Ultimately, Bonafon's missives to her contacts at court proved successful as she was released from the convent in 1760 and, remarkably, provided a pension by the king of the not inconsiderable sum of 300 livres a year, which she enjoyed until the end of her life in 1770.

Bonafon's *Tanastès* is an allegorical fantasy story about the eponymous character, a prince of the Zarimois, who takes several mistresses during his adventures. The character Tanastès was obviously intended to represent King Louis XV. Not leaving the proper identification of the dramatis personae to chance, the published novel was sold with a key indicating the real-life counterparts of the fictional characters. This key was found later in the investigation and led the investigator (police chief Marville) to the conclusion that Bonafon was indeed responsible for the novel. *Tanastès* was sold surreptitiously but spread widely enough that Louis' own daughter, Princess Adélaïde, came into possession of a copy. At the time of her arrest, Bonafon had written other works, including poetry, an unfinished historical novel called *Le Baron de XXX*, and three plays: *Le Destin*, *Les Dons*, and *Le Demi-Savant*. Bonafon later published another novel, *Confidences d'une jolie femme* (*Secrets of a Pretty Woman*), in 1747. The whereabouts of these manuscripts, if they survive, are unknown, and locating them would be a worthy goal for further research.[4]

The Publication and Subsequent Legal Process

The legal brief of Bonafon's arrest, interrogation, and subsequent legal actions is preserved in the Archives de la Bastille and is the central focus of this study. These documents illuminate Bonafon's story and provide context for understanding her intentions. Though she was refused pen and paper from the start of the proceedings, several handwritten letters by Bonafon herself remain in the file. These writings reveal her strategy of self-protection and suggest the rebellious nature of *Tanastès*, while underscoring the importance of the gender and social class of the writer.

Through the legal instrument of the *lettre de cachet*, a mechanism officially bearing the imprimatur of the king, Bonafon was held in the Bastille for fourteen months, remaining in prison throughout the period of the formal investigation and interrogation.[5] In fact, when she became frail, she wrote letters to Duval, the secretary of police, who communicated with the police chief, Marville. Bonafon developed an epistolary relationship with Duval through her letter writing. There is also evidence that the powerful Cardinal Joly de Fleury intervened, and Bonafon managed to be moved to le couvent des Bernardines de Moulins near Vichy, France. That Bonafon was released from the Bastille and consigned to a convent was a significant accomplishment. The conditions of her confinement there were certainly much better than at the Bastille. There she remained until her release in 1760. While in the convent, Bonafon was still to be deprived of pen and paper and precluded from writing.[6] Despite the official restriction, Bonafon did continue to write letters between 1748 and 1751. This fact is documented by the several examples found in her file dating to 1745–1759. These letters are of central interest to this study and help to fill out the story of her writing "career." We may regard Bonafon's letters from prison as another notable act of empowerment through writing (the first being her novel that got her into trouble).

There is no evidence that an actual trial ever took place. Instead, there are detailed records of the interrogation, and each folio is stamped with the official court seal. The investigation is marked by stages: 1) Discovery, 2) Interrogation, and finally, 3) Confrontation. Bonafon was held in the Bastille for the period of the interrogation and then consigned to remain there at the conclusion of this process. Bonafon was sentenced, confined, and ordered to remain "*embastillée*" until "the crown should decide to release her."[7]

Social Media and Police Discovery of *Tanastès*: Bonafon Arrested

Much gossip was generated by reading the publicized information from the legal briefs. They were often discussed in public, in cafés and salons. This type of spreading of information played a significant role in the lead-up to the Revolution. According to Darnton: "In August of 1745 the police discover a recent clandestinely published book in the form of a fairy tale that seems to reveal King Louis XV's love-life."[8] The police investigation into the novel resulted in the arrest of 21 booksellers, publishers, and others, including Bonafon herself in August 1745. The police chief, Marville, did his work and discovered the provenance of the book, which led him to a chambermaid, Mlle Bonafon, who served the Princesse de Montauban. That Bonafon was interrogated by Claude Henri Feydeau de Marville, the lieutenant general of police, indicates the importance Bonafon's work held and the perceived danger of her publication to the court. Marville had doubts about Bonafon's ability to compose literary fantasies based on the intrigues of the court, even though she had a front-seat view of all the goings-on. She had witnessed the fall of (*la favorite*) Chateauroux and the rise of Mme de Pompadour as Louis XV's court mistress and would have been well aware of the delicate nature of this transition.[9] As Pompadour was also a very shrewd politician in her own way, she was already trying to align herself with all the people who were important and rising to power at court. She was a supporter of Marville and therefore he "needed to prevent the inner workings of the court from being exposed to the public."[10] The Marquise de Pompadour was also acutely aware of how gossip could damage the court and, more importantly, her reputation.[11]

According to much of the testimony in the file, Marville kept his investigation focused on the others involved in the case. He also circled back to the idea that the publication of the novel was accompanied by a key, and he implied that Bonafon certainly would have been involved in writing this important connecting piece of the novel.[12] Though Bonafon admitted to having written the novel, she denied any intention of damaging the court.

The title *Tanastès* is an obvious anagram of *Satan est*, which is Latin, and *est Satan* which is French for "is Satan." Inventing or composing a title such as *Tanastès* as a derogatory anagram representing the king becomes a central part of this discussion and analysis, especially when speaking about the context of the work's creation and the author's aims. It is worth noting that historians have alerted readers to the art of decoding while reading this text.[13] Deciphering anagrams was part of the intrigue of reading, including titles, character names, and keys. *Tanastès*, in fact, suggests and reinforces the devilish nature of the king's behavior.[14] The author appears to have been highly focused on criticizing the king's behavior, and therefore found a way to present his personality in a defensible manner (perhaps in case she was to be caught—which was highly likely). According to the record, the arrest only occurred because of the content of the novel. Lisa Jane Graham suggests that the approach Bonafon took in the novel, of using two opposing sides of the personality of Louis XV, may have been to "humanize" the king and demonstrate the fact that all humans are composed of good and evil.[15] One does have to question what gave a servant of the court the taste for such risky writing?[16]

In any case, it is important to acknowledge Bonafon's tenacity and intelligence, and perhaps to consider the expressed view of her intentions. Eventually, Marville confronted all those accused and was able, at least, to undermine Bonafon's story by counting the numbers of copies that were printed and sold. The record shows that 200 copies of *Tanastès* were published, and that quantity was significant enough to cause great concern for the Crown. When the distribution was halted, only 45 copies had been sold. However, this was sufficient for damage to be done. It may have been that the king changed strategy. The first impulse was to appear secure enough to treat this "woman's threat" like a mosquito bite, a minor and insignificant criticism of no consequence or threat to his position. The police response was, if not draconian, at least rather vigorous, bearing witness to the popularity of the novel, or at least its content and the scandal surrounding it. Ultimately, Bonafon was punished as she was found guilty of "producing and distributing the most dangerous and disrespectful kind of literature."[17]

The way Bonafon conducted herself throughout her imprisonment (the move from prison to the convent and then her strategy leading towards her own liberation) demonstrates a form of resistance writing. It is one way that the "chambermaid-come-author" theme resonates with us today. We can also consider this story of a "resister" within the larger narrative of women's growing political role in the eighteenth-century French context.[18] Bonafon wrote a novel impugning the king, and while it is true that most critics do not consider Bonafon's literary work to be of great consequence or influence (there has been a bit of scholarly commentary about the poor literary quality of her writing), the political aims of the work seem increasingly important.[19] As the title and the interrogation materials provided by Bonafon's testimony suggest a more direct attack on the king than previously thought, we are left to wonder if Bonafon was really so oblivious to the potential consequences of her writing that she risked her freedom to compose and publish her work.

Bonafon's careful denials and replies to her interrogators implied a deeper understanding of her offense. In the legal briefs of Bonafon's interrogation, we can gain respect for her perspicacity and ability to confound and outwit her interrogators. According to Darnton, Bonafon worked the police chief, Marville, into a great frenzy.[20] He arrested everybody involved in the case, including a young boy selling lemonade outside the publisher's office. Darnton recounts:

> Marville laid traps; Mlle de Bonafon tried to avoid them; and the transcript of the interrogation recorded all of their moves, for it was written in the form of a dialogue: question-answer, question-answer, each page initialed by Mlle Bonafon as testimony to its accuracy.[21]

Because Bonafon had already penned a few books by the time she was discovered by the police, we can assume she must have been prepared in some way for this moment. But if she had "appeared" to prepare a defense, it would make her seem naïve.

Let us remember that women who were lettered often had a modicum of formal education. Most were autodidacts and were not latinized. Previous research by Dena Goodman and Janet Altman suggests that the reading materials available to women were mainly restricted to letters, lists, and, if they were lucky, a few novels, though women did have limited access to educational tools and tutelage in convents.[22] Nevertheless, one should not take at face value Bonafon's claims to her interrogators that she had no tutelage or help in writing books, and that the works were produced out of whole cloth from her own creativity and imagination. Darnton highlights Bonafon's dramatic encounter with the chief of police:

> It was an extraordinary moment: a female servant telling the head of police force, one of the most powerful men in the

> kingdom, that she had written a novel because she wanted to write a novel and that she had done it on her own, without help from anyone. The lieutenant general could not take it in.[23]

It appears that what made Bonafon's work so threatening was the idea that many were involved in its dissemination, having the marks of a conspiracy or larger movement. There were those individuals she had to protect; those who helped with the publication, sale, and distribution, as well as the provision of the key that accompanied the book to help readers identify the characters with actual personages at court. At first in the interviews with police chief Marville, Bonafon worked hard to avoid implicating others involved in the case. The key, the title, the preface, and the original epitaph demonstrated a higher level of Latin education than expected from a woman of Bonafon's station. Bonafon's education may not have included a deep grounding in Latin letters, and that implies she might have had help with these parts when writing *Tanastès*.[24] It could alternately imply that she did have a deeper grasp of Latin and written French than scholars in the past have assumed. As we eventually learn, the valet, Mazilin, admitted to having been Bonafon's accomplice and to having written the Latin epitaph.[25]

Graham has suggested that *Tanastès*, contrary to some previous claims, exhibits many "literary" qualities.[26] In fact, quite a few romans-à-clef were written about King Louis XV at the time of Bonafon's work, and regarding this rather widespread phenomenon, Graham writes: "Many directed this attention towards the crown, others experimented with new genres such as the novel, that enabled self-expression and criticism."[27] This supports the idea that Bonafon could very well have used the excuse of the king being a bestselling subject. On the other hand, we continue to ask, why would her attack be so direct and obvious if not to impugn the king?[28] Throughout the proceedings, Bonafon maintained that *Tanastès* was just a fairy story and not intended to be about King Louis XV, despite the presence of the key included in the publication identifying the king and several courtiers. Bonafon used this device to criticize Louis XV without attacking him directly, because Louis XV was, in effect, both kings.

Nowhere in the recorded proceedings was Bonafon asked about the title, nor did she ever disclose her purpose as anything other than "making money." In fact, Bonafon consistently expressed a purely pecuniary motive for her literary exploits, explaining that she wished to make money from the sale of her book and that she had no desire to damage the king's reputation. Marville relentlessly attacked Bonafon's defense, seeking a full confession, but ended up relying on indirect evidence to try to prove Bonafon's motives and intentions. This most damning evidence revolved around the question of the key. The key was problematic, in that it indicated that Bonafon did have collaborators, at least in bringing the work to press and distributing it. The belief that Bonafon could not have acted alone may have worked in her favor, as Marville was not inclined to give Bonafon much credit as an author or independent creator since he could not accept that a woman, and a servant at that, could compose such a story. Perhaps he was seeking to expose a "bigger fish," possibly someone of higher status at the court. Marville's bias against a woman writer served as a backhanded compliment, as if to say that if her writing was good enough to be considered a man's work—it must have had some literary merit.

Confronted with the facts at hand, Bonafon modified her responses in interrogation. Marville had done his research, but Bonafon never admitted to trying to slander the king directly. Yet, as the testimonial record shows, she repeated that she only intended to make money and that the king's intrigues seemed to be of great interest and would therefore sell books. She stated to Marville that injuring the king's reputation was never her direct intention. Yet, the title of the novel, *Tanastès,* I would argue, reinforces the idea that her first intent was to attack the king. In the end the interrogation transcript reads, "She had tried to enrich herself by slandering the crown."[29] She was not accused of a direct violent threat to the king, and not sentenced to death. Perhaps her "literary sword" was not sharp enough to inflict more than a minor pinprick on the king, though it seems, in retrospect, that Bonafon's intent was sharper than her consequent punishment would suggest.

A central question, both for the police investigation and for historians, is that of Bonafon's true motivation in writing and publishing the work. Was Bonafon mainly seeking financial gain and, having access to the court, using her knowledge of the intrigues there to cater to an always avid interest in court gossip and scandal? Or, alternatively, did Bonafon have a more political purpose in writing a thinly veiled critique of a lustful monarch and court riven by subterfuge and self-serving acts? Was she simply feeding an insatiable appetite for gossip on the part of the public, or serving up an unattractive portrayal of some at court to benefit others, perhaps a patron or friend of higher status? In any case, it seems the publication of the novel was a grave miscalculation for Bonafon. The novel was seen as going far beyond what was considered acceptable humor.

Précis of the Novel

The prince (Tanastès, or Louis XV according to the key) is born in the land of the Zarimois (the French). A sylph snatches the baby prince and delivers him to the care of his tutor (Oromal, or the Cardinal de Fleury), who is to instruct the lad until he is ready to ascend to the throne. Meanwhile, an evil lookalike (Agamil) is substituted for the prince. He gives free rein to his lust as he grows up, while Tanastès observes indignantly from above, seated on a cloud. Agamil takes up with "an antique fairy" (Mme de Mailly, who is represented as good-natured, and is Louis XV's first mistress among the daughters of the marquis de Nesle). The antique fairy is able to minimize the damage to the kingdom. But then Agamil (the evil lookalike) exchanges her for a better-looking mistress (Mme de Lauragais, daughter number two), and finally settles on a third, passionate, scheming femme fatale, "Ardentine" (Mme de Chateauroux, daughter number three), who makes Agamil her slave as he becomes a tyrant ruling over the kingdom. When a war breaks out, Agamil goes off to fight at the front, and Ardentine follows him. On her way, she encounters the good king, Tanastès, whom she takes at first to be Agamil; but when she makes advances towards him, he scorns her. As she is turned away, she returns to the court and, in a fit of rage, with the help of a magic wand, banishes everyone to a hellish underground kingdom of gnomes. At this moment, the climax of the story, the supreme sylph (Amariel, the bishop of Soissons) intervenes. He arms Tanastès with magic lightning and sends him to rescue the court. Tanastès routs the gnomes; the bad king is transformed into a snake; the wicked mistress swallows the snake and as it gnaws at her entrails, she is banished to the underground. The good king is reunited with the queen (thanks to some bedroom magic performed by the sylphs, they had been spending the nights together and the days apart). The bad king, Agamil, is enslaved to his scheming mistress, Ardentine, and cedes all control to her. The royal couple persevere in the second half; they appear ready to rule happily ever after but meet with some more minor adventures, and the fairy tale ends.[30]

Intertextuality and Theatricality

Robert Darnton's insistence on the intertexuality of the piece may lead us also to ask the question of whether or not *Tanastès* may have been shaped to be performed as a drama. The fluid nature of performative works and their ability to extend their reach with the public in many forms has been explored by Darnton in his many works. We note that in the novel, each character has a role and speaks. Perhaps the line between novel and play is not entirely distinct. Bonafon's work could have become even more dangerous and impactful if had been performed before an audience, rather than being read in private. It is possible that the work's potential performativity made it especially threatening to those in power.

Extending his analysis to "mixed media" such as gossip and song, Darnton emphasizes that the spread of the message, how it reached the public and took hold, mattered more than where it originated in sociocultural terms.[31] The novel *Tanastès* if performed could take the themes of the court from oral to written, and from written to printed, back to oral again. The play is written in part as an interior monologue. It seems to assume a public and has performative content. In this highly dramatic and potentially theatrical piece, Bonafon transmuted the dynamics of courtly life into a piquant mythical farce.[32]

Antimonarchical Epistolarity: The Letters and the Problematics

Bonafon produced a body of correspondence from prison and convent, including at least 20 personal handwritten letters with police secretary Duval and the Monseigneur from 1745–1757. It is significant that Bonafon was forbidden to "write" at all, and yet here we have evidence of a daring communication that may have reached the ear of the king. It is as if the very act of a woman's skillful writing, not only its content, drew the attention of the king, the police, and all others involved. The reaction to Bonafon's work may be seen as an all-encompassing commentary on women's writing as an act of empowerment. Her letters were often written as a dialogue between two people and seemed to reflect the awareness of a public reader. Curiously in an attempt to suppress dissent, the letters of dissidents once confiscated and opened by the king's police were not destroyed but made available to the public. Marville thought that every dimension of the act must be criticized in order to shut it down.

Literary Production and Notes from Bonafon to M. Duval, Secretary of Police

The question of literary production is very significant when it comes to the letters that Bonafon wrote to keep her network alive. The question of "literariness" or literary style takes on central importance in this discussion. In the plea-letter figured below, the formulaic greetings are present, as is the careful disclosure of personal sentiment. Thus, establishing an intimacy of sorts with the recipient, M. Duval, Secretary of Police.

The epistolary medium of expression gave women access to a larger public forum. It is often claimed by some scholars of the eighteenth century that letter writing was a feminine form of writing. Janet Altman counters the claim and links epistolarity to the gendering of letter writing.[33] More letters were indeed written by women at the time, but that does not mean that letter writing was restricted to communication between women or that the subject of the letters was domestic in nature. Bonafon wrote of this issue herself in the eighteenth century and spoke of the crucial nature of being able to express herself by letters to the Monseigneur:

> *Souf[f]rez Monseigneur que je vous rappelle les ordres qui furent donnes y à mon arrivée, je dois rendre compte ils de tout le papier qu'on me donnera cela me semble renfermer une permission tacite d'en avoir je m'en suis cependant point? prévalué? et n'en ay demande quelques feuilles que lesquelles m'ont été absolument nécessaires et jamais pour mon amusement, qu'oy qu'à dire vrai cette ressource ne me serait guère moins favorable que la bastille ou l'on avait bien voulu me la permettre. Dites moy donc je vous justifier sy j'en suis faire usage soit pour copier soit pour mettre mes propres idées…*

> Attention Monsieur I remind you that the orders that were given upon my arrival were to give back all the paper and to shut me away with tacit permission, I didn't even ask for the few pages that were absolutely necessary to me and not for my amusement, but this solution is much better even though in the Bastille, they may have permitted me pen and paper. Tell me then how you justify what I may use in order to copy my own ideas…

Bonafon continued to underscore the importance of writing her ideas in the same letter:

> *Dites moy donc je vous justifier sy j'en suis faire usage soit pour copier soit pour mettre mes propres idées par écrit aux conditions de m'en sortir aucune de la maison de ne les y communiquer a personne si ce n'est pas à mon confesseur, de les bruler ensuite ou de les remettre à la supérieure et le tout par compte.*
>
> Tell me then if I were to justify [having pen and paper] to write these ideas, either for using them or for writing my own thoughts in order to help end or consignment, they are not written to communicate with anyone, even if it is only to my confessor none of these letters would be seen, they would be burned afterwards or put into the hands of the mother superior.[34]

Letters, therefore, were not only a part of a purely personal sort of communication within the private sphere of women. Once within the legal process, whether intended or not, many letters were read by lawyers and others looking at the brief, often making this literature available to the public. According to Altman, letter writing was public, and it did not matter whether it was intended for publication or not. Bonafon's letters over the span of many years show us a level of persistence and resistance that proved an even more dangerous example, and it is worth repeating here that as part of her sentence she was deprived of pen and paper and confined to a solitary life.

Bonafon had begun to develop her letters, as she demonstrated a cultivated "naturalness" accorded to women of the era. This standard is clarified in Dena Goodman's work, *Becoming a Woman in the Age of Letters*, when we are looking at the "naturalness" that had been cultivated in the minds of women for their letter writing. Many have looked to Mme de Sévigné in the previous century to define the "feminine epistolary style" as the "aesthetic of negligence." Here Goodman writes:

> The skills to write not just a letter, but an elegant letter, an appropriate letter, the kind of letter that was said to come naturally to women, had to be acquired. However, in the eighteenth century there was no established system of education and no standard instruction for girls.[35]

Literate women had, by necessity, honed their skills at letter writing. The very act of writing is what makes it a feminist/dissident act, an act of resistance. Outside the drama of *Tanastès*, the "roman-à-clef," there are dimensions of resistance in the letters written from inside the prison and the convent. Bonafon, from prison and convent, produced a body of correspondence, including at least 20 personal handwritten letters with Duval from 1745–1757. Normally, the letters in a friendly correspondence would include what Goodman would refer to as "an orality." Most of the dissident letters that Bonafon wrote (amongst others) are contrite and urgent. We never forget that they were addressed, for the most part, to members of the patriarchy. Janet Altman says that there is a determinative femininity to contrition and addressing the sovereign. Bonafon models this tone of contrition and adopts a subservient "feminity" in her tone in order to be effective.

Strategy and Networking in Bonafon's Letters

The politics of recourse through the epistolary approach can be complicated, but Bonafon was up to the task. Bonafon certainly must have felt an allegiance to her mistress, Princess Montauban, and she most certainly heard the court gossip from the princess and absorbed information about the rising power of the new love interest of the king, the Marquise de Pompadour. She tried through her network to convey her message to the king's mistress. In this excerpt, she was writing to her aunt to write directly to the Marquise de Pompadour to try to gain favor in the eyes of the king:

J'ay fait une faute j'en suis punie rien n'est plus juste. Mais vous savez Madame la marquise de Pompadour tient actuellement dans le monde je suis sure qu'une lettre de vous favorise beaucoup auprès d'elle un mot d'elle seroit tout pour moi.

I committed an error and I have been punished and nothing is more correct. But you know Madame la Marquise de Pompadour has [all the power] in the world and I am sure that a letter from you will put me in her favor and a word from her would be everything for me.

J'aime le roi de tout mon cœur et je ne connais pas comment j'ay put dire quelque chose qui lui offense c'est une faute d'imagination plutôt que d'une volonté déterminée mais ce n'est pas vue aussi bien est-ce un pardon que je demande et non vue une justice écrivez-vous ma chère tante faut-il que je vous interprète par la peinture de mon état?

I love the king with all my heart and I don't know how I could have said anything that would offend him, if at all it is a fault of my imagination rather than one of my determined will but it is not only a pardon that I am asking for, nor am I asking for a different form of justice for which I write you my dear aunt, I just ask if you could paint the picture of my state of being at this time to her [so that it may be conveyed to the king].

Votre très humble et très obéissante servante, Bonafon

Your very humble and very obedient servant, Bonafon

Je ne sais s'il vous me permis de montrer ma lettre mais cela sait ou non ne la montrer point pour l'amour du moy tout le monde n'est pas vous et n'a pas votre tendresse que tout cecy soit sous le sceau du décret. Je crois que l'adresse de Mme de Pompadour et au château à Versailles.

I do not know if he will permit you to show my letter but that know or not for you to show her for love of me no one is like you, they do not know your kindness, and all this is under the seal of the king. I think the address of the Marquise de Pompadour is at the Palace of Versailles.[36]

The post scriptum indicated Bonafon's strong desire and anticipation that there would be an audience for her letters since she was told she would not have access to pen or paper. She also showed her deep knowledge of the inner workings of the court and a strategy to gain access to the king. Here Bonafon's strategy was to create a line of communication through women to get to the king. She was writing to a woman (her aunt) in order to communicate with the king's new mistress (Pompadour). The voice and tone were not the same she would later use in the letters to Marville and Duval. The language was not ingratiating, except for the formulaic ending, which seems to endorse the notion that she was aware that her readership would be more than just her aunt.

In the following letter (Figures 3.1–3.3), Bonafon took a clear risk and tried to further sway the king by attempting to communicate with the Marquise de Pompadour via Duval.[37]

> *Monseigneur,*
> *La réputation de clémence et de bonté que vous vous êtes sy justement acquise et les effets que j'en ay resentay par moi-même depuis ma détention me donnent la confiance d'oser vous demander une grâce, d'où dépend je crois ma liberté et peut sauver ma vie puisque je sens qu'il m'est impossible de vivre encore lontems (longtemps) prisonnière et haie de personnes du monde que je respecte le plus sincèrement/ (page suivante… ne suit pas directement).*
>
> *Permettez moy donc je vous supplie de travailler à réparer ma faute, (souffrez)/sachez que je recherche le recours de Madame la marquise de Pompadour et peut adoucir l'esprit du roy en luy peignant toute ma douleur, j'ay en l'honneur d'estre connue d'elle autrefois mais vue toute que j'ai à Saint Joseph l'est encore plus particulièrement que moy je suis persuadée qu'elle ne refuserait pas a sa prière de s'intervenir en ma faveur et j'ay hazardé (hasardé) d'écrirse pour cela a ma tante dans l'espérance que vous voudriez bien lui faire ma lettre, au nom de Monseigneur ne me refusez pas ajouter cette grâce à toutes celles que j'ai déjà reçues de vous. S'il ne faut qu'être malheureuse et repentante pour mériter votre protection personne en vérité ne la mérite plus que moy, je suis avec vos très profond respect.*
>
> *Monseigneur*
> *Votre très humble et très obéissante servante,*
> *Bonafon*

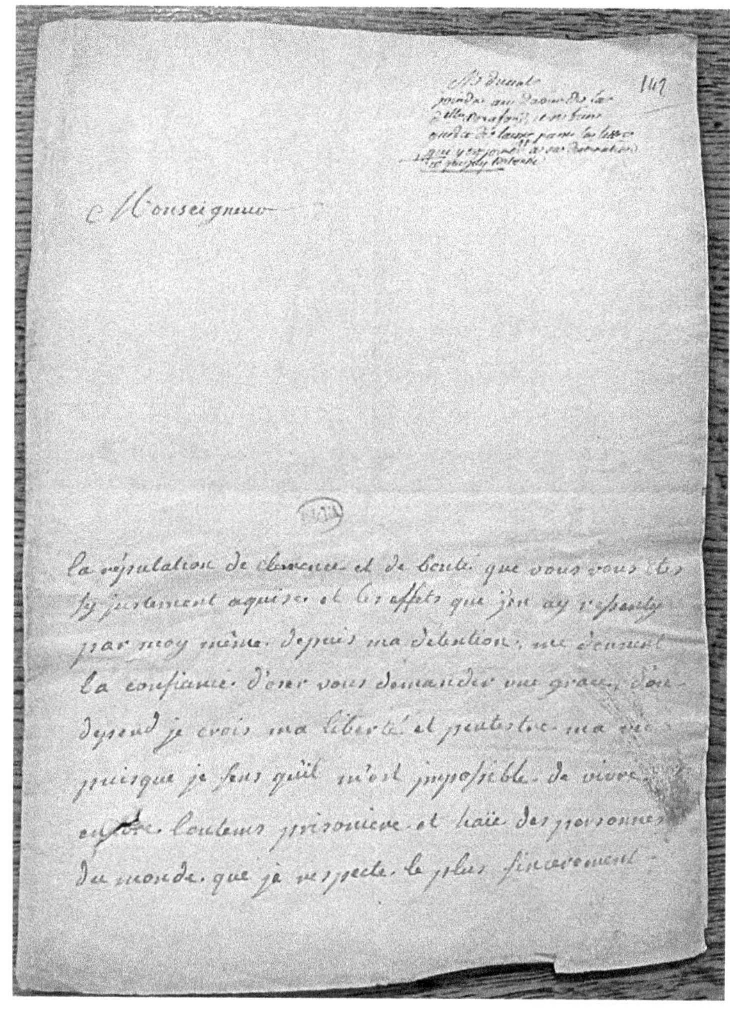

Monseigneur

la réputation de clémence et de bonté que vous vous êtes
si justement acquise, et les effets que j'en ay ressentis
par moy même depuis ma détention, me donnent
la confiance d'oser vous demander une grâce, d'où
dépend je crois ma liberté et peutêtre ma vie
puisque je sens qu'il m'est impossible de vivre
encore longtems prisoniere et haïe des personnes
du monde que je respecte le plus sincerement.

Figure 3.1 Page one of letter from Bonafon to Duval. Photograph by the author.

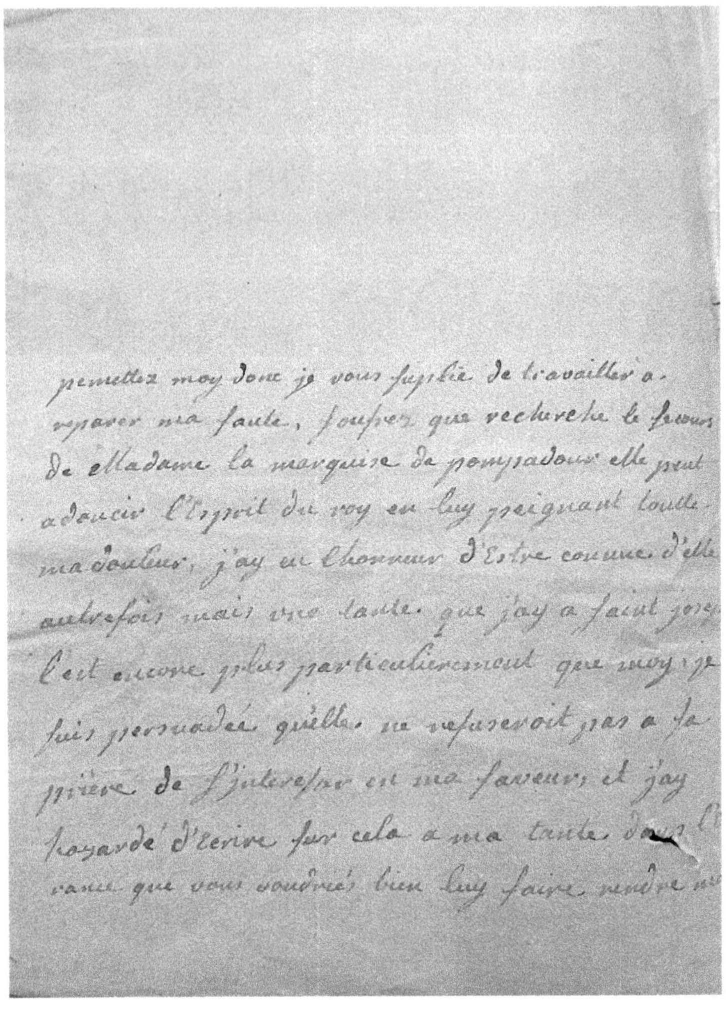

permettez moy donc je vous supplie de travailler a
reparer ma faute, souffrez que recherche la faveur
de Madame la marquise de pompadour elle peut
adoucir l'esprit du roy en luy peignant toutte
ma douleur, j'ay eu l'honneur d'Estre connue d'elle
autrefois mais une tante que jay a faint jose
l'est encore plus particulierement que moy, je
suis persuadée quelle ne refuseroit pas a sa
priere de s'interesser en ma faveur, et jay
hasardé d'ecrire sur cela a ma tante dans
rance que vous voudrés bien luy faire rendre

Figure 3.2 Source: AB, MS 11582, 147. Page two of letter from Bonafon to Duval. Photograph by the author.

Source: AB, MS 11582, 148.

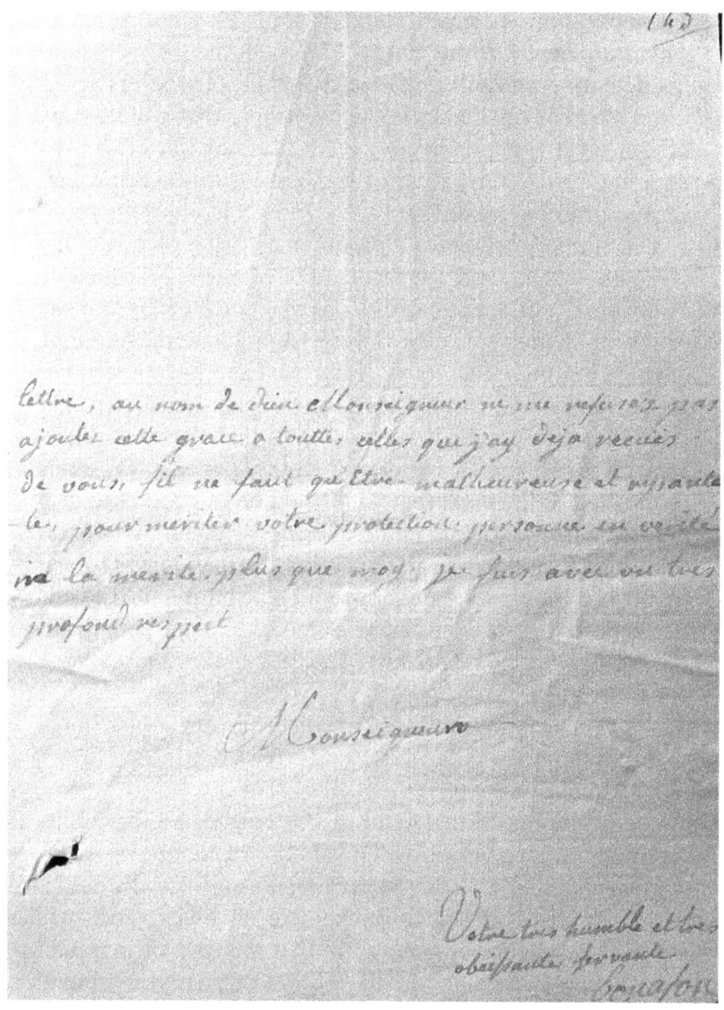

lettre, au nom de dieu Monseigneur ne me refusez pas
ajoutez cette grace a toutte celles que j'ay deja receües
de vous, s'il ne faut qu'etre malheureuse et repentan
-te, pour meriter votre protection personne en verité
na la merite plus que moy. je suis avec un tres
profond respect

Monseigneur

Votre tres humble et tres
obeissante servante
Bonafon

Figure 3.3 Page three of letter from Bonafon to Duval. Photograph by the author.

Source: AB, MS 11582, 149.

Monseigneur,
The reputation of clemency and of goodness and their effect which you have justly acquired, I have felt them myself since my detention and this gives me the confidence to ask you a favor, whereas my liberty is the only thing that will save my life since I it is impossible for me to live any longer as prisoner and to feel the hatred of the persons in the world that I respect most sincerely.

Therefore, I beg you to permit me to try to repair my error, know that I seek the recourse of Mme the Marquise de Pompadour and she can soften the spirit of the king and she can paint all my pain and sadness to him, I have the honor of having been presented to her in the past and having seen her particularly at St. Joseph, that I myself am persuaded that she will not refuse me her prayers and that she could intervene on my behalf. I have also taken the chance to write this to my aunt in the hope that you would be so good as to give my letter to her. In the name of "Monseigneur" please do not forget to add this to all the graces you have already given to me. If it is only to be unhappy and repentant to merit your protection, no one would merit it more than me, yours with the most profound respect.

Monseigneur,
Your very humble and very obedient servant,
Bonafon[38]

Only the beginning of this letter can be considered formulaic, as Bonafon ingratiated herself to Duval: "*La réputation de clémence et de bonté que vous vous êtes sy justement acquise…*" I would also suggest that this is a signature example of what Nancy Miller refers to as a "poetics of gender," in that the style of ingratiation was particularly "female" in its required structures.[39] Bonafon stated that Duval had a reputation for goodness and clemency and that she herself had experienced this with him, so dared to ask a large favor of him. She then wasted no time, moving directly to put forward her audacious request, which was to put a good word in the ear of the Marquise de Pompadour, and in turn to ask that the marquise put a good word in for Bonafon with the king. It seems that Bonafon's strategy of transmitting her plea through the most powerful woman in France, and the person with the most access to the king, was rather brilliant. It may also illustrate the mechanisms of feminine power in that setting. In this missive, Bonafon established sympathy with the secretary of police, but not with Marville himself since she knew the latter had already worked the interrogation and found her guilty. Also, Marville was working hard to remain in the good graces of Pompadour because of her power at court. So, Bonafon chose the second in line, and it was a good choice at that.[40]

Darnton's initial assessment of how to read the letters and testimony proves problematic: "One cannot read them literally. But, however biased, they provide accounts of the tone, the place, and the participants of the talk, they include information about information."[41] In the years 1745–1746/7 (14 months in the Bastille), we can see how the content of the letters' language evolved.[42] Even though Bonafon's health was poor, we see consistency in the way the polite formula of address was repeated. As Bonafon's pleas became more urgent, the language became sophisticated and more formulaic. It is of note, however, that the postscripts were hurried and often misspelled, perhaps indicating the level of feeling with which she concluded her letter. In the above letter, she asked to be consigned to the convent, perhaps a moment of this communication that showed audacity and a level of empowerment, perhaps knowing her life depended on the plea made in the letter she sent.[43] While it may be difficult to untangle Bonafon's intentions and motivations in writing and publishing *Tanastès*, the skill and persistence of her campaign to free herself from the consequences are quite clear.[44]

> *Monseigneur, Quoy que les bontés dont vous m'avez honorée jusqu'icy m'ayant suspire la plus vive reconnaissance il me semble que je vous l'ay toujours marquée sy faiblement que je me reproche sous cela d'avoir paru s'y peu sensible à toute de grâces, j'ose dire cependant que la seule timidité retenoit les expressions que mon cœur me dictait devant vous le respect l'emportoit pour la confiance à présent je les sens également souffres donc monseigneur que je sens vous fatiguer par des remerciements importunes.*
>
> Monseigneur, Whatever the goodness with which you honor me until now, it inspires my deepest recognition, and it seems that I have been weak in my acknowledgment of that. I reproach myself if I have seemed insensitive or ungrateful,

therefore I dare to say with only timidity that holds back the deeper and heartfelt expressions. I would also like to show you respect, so that lends me to think that I may tire you with my excessive expressions of gratitude.

Je profite de la liberté que je vous dois pour vous assurer quelquefois de tout ce que je peux ressentir une personne extrêmement reconnaissante envers un protecteur infiniment généreux je finis avec un profond respect et la plus parfaite soumission.

I benefit from the liberty that I owe to you, in order to reassure you that all that I feel I am someone who is extremely grateful to an infinitely generous protector, and I close with an expression of my profound respect and my most perfect submission.

Du couvent des dames Bernardines
A Moulins ce 10 fevrier 1747
Monseigneur,
Votre humble et obéissante servante,
Bonafon

From the Convent of the Bernardines
At Moulins this 10th of February 1747[45]

Monseigneur le major ayant eu la bonté de me remettre mes hardes votre ordre est je crois la seule chose qui me retient actuellement à la Bastille, je pense que le retardement que vous apportez à mon départ es d'une nouvelle obligatoire que je vous ay ma faiblesse et la mauvaise saison excitent votre pitié pour moy et je suis tellement pénétrée de reconnaissance pour tant de marques de bonté que je ne sais en quel termes l'exprimer mais après vous avoir fait mes très humbles remerciements, j'ose vous faire remarquer que le temps et à présent plus doux que nous ne devons l'attendre de plus d'un mois au moins que ma faute ruinée a besoin d'un prompt remède pour la rétablir et qu'il n'en est point assurément de plus efficace que ma sortie la rigueur du froid n'ayant rien de comparable à l'ennuy qui me consume, sy donc je me rends point importance pour trop de précipitation et considérant la tristesse de mon état vous vouliez bien monseigneur hâter le moment de ma liberté ce fera un surcroise de

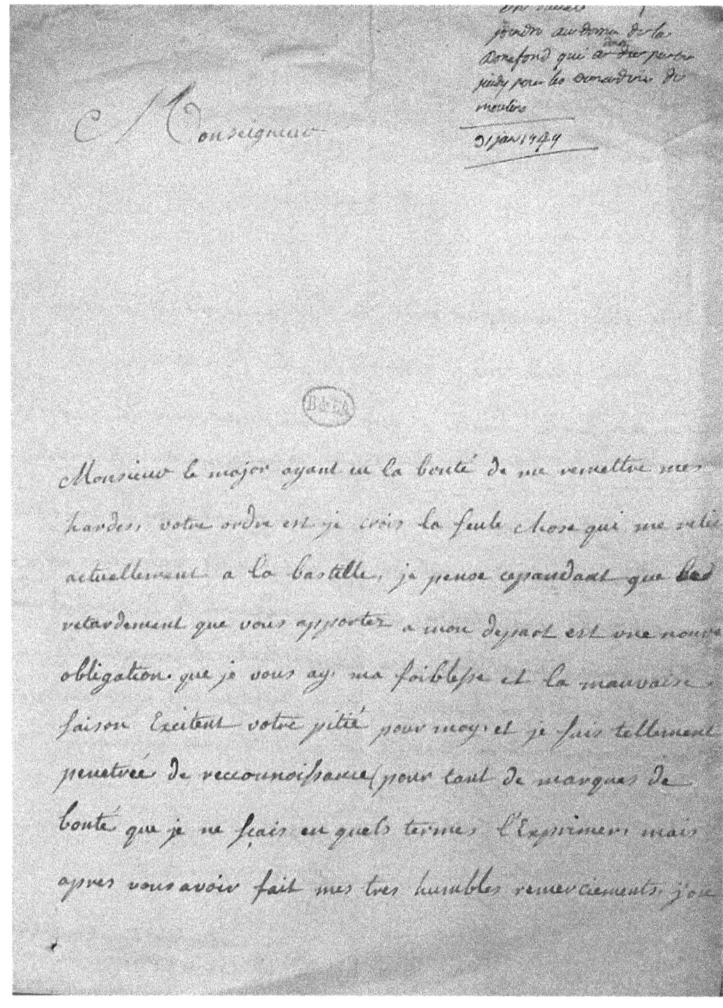

Monseigneur

Monsieur le major ayant eu la bonté de me remettre mes
hardes, votre ordre est je crois la seule chose qui me retie[nt]
actuellement a la bastille, je pense cependant que le
retardement que vous apporter a mon depart est une nouv[elle]
obligation que je vous ay, ma foiblesse et la mauvaise
saison Excitent votre pitié pour moy, et je suis tellement
penetrée de reconnoissance pour tout de marques de
bonté que je ne sçais en quels termes l'Exprimer, mais
apres vous avoir fait mes tres humbles remerciements, j'ose

Figure 3.4 Page one of letter from Bonafon to the Monseigneur (Cardinal de Rohan). Photograph by the author

Source: AB, MS 11582, 149..

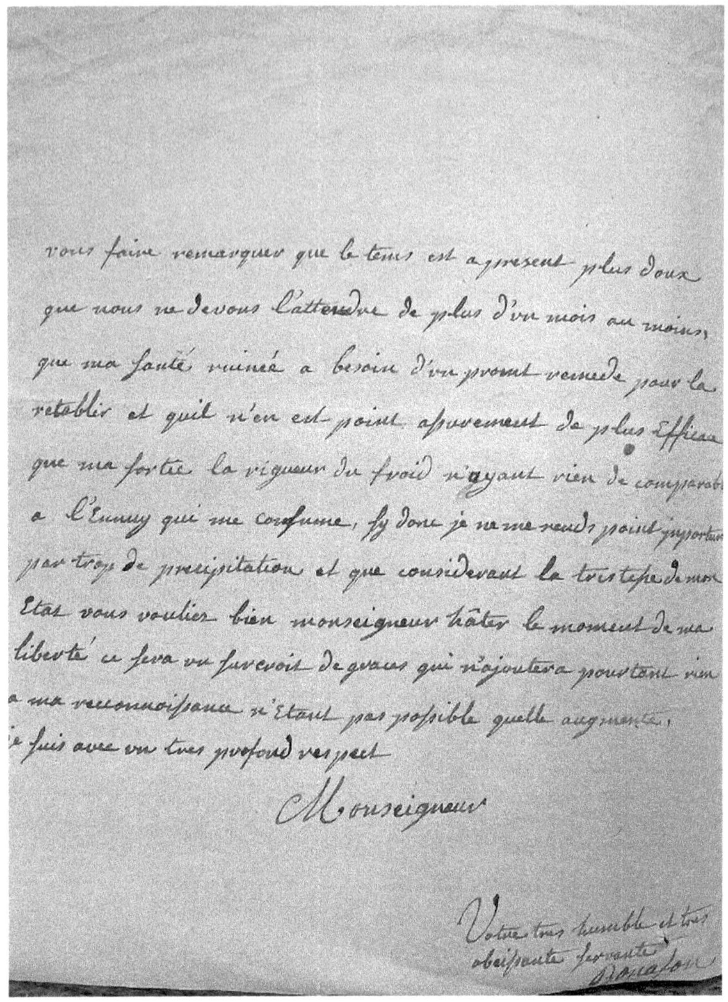

vous faire remarquer que le tems est a present plus doux
que nous ne devons l'attendre de plus d'un mois au moins,
que ma santé ruinée a besoin d'un promt remede pour la
retablir et quil n'en est point assurement de plus Efficace
que ma sortie la vigueur du froid n'ayant rien de comparab
a l'Ennuy qui me consume, si donc je ne me rends point importun
par trop de precipitation et que considerant la tristesse de mon
Etat vous vouliez bien monseigneur hâter le moment de ma
liberté ce sera un surcroit de graces qui n'ajoutera pourtant rien
a ma reconnoissance n'Etant pas possible quelle augmente,
je suis avec un tres profond respect

Monseigneur

Votre tres humble et tres
obeissante servante
Bonafon

Figure 3.5 Page two of letter from Bonafon to the Monseigneur. Photograph by the author.

Source: AB, MS 11582, 149.

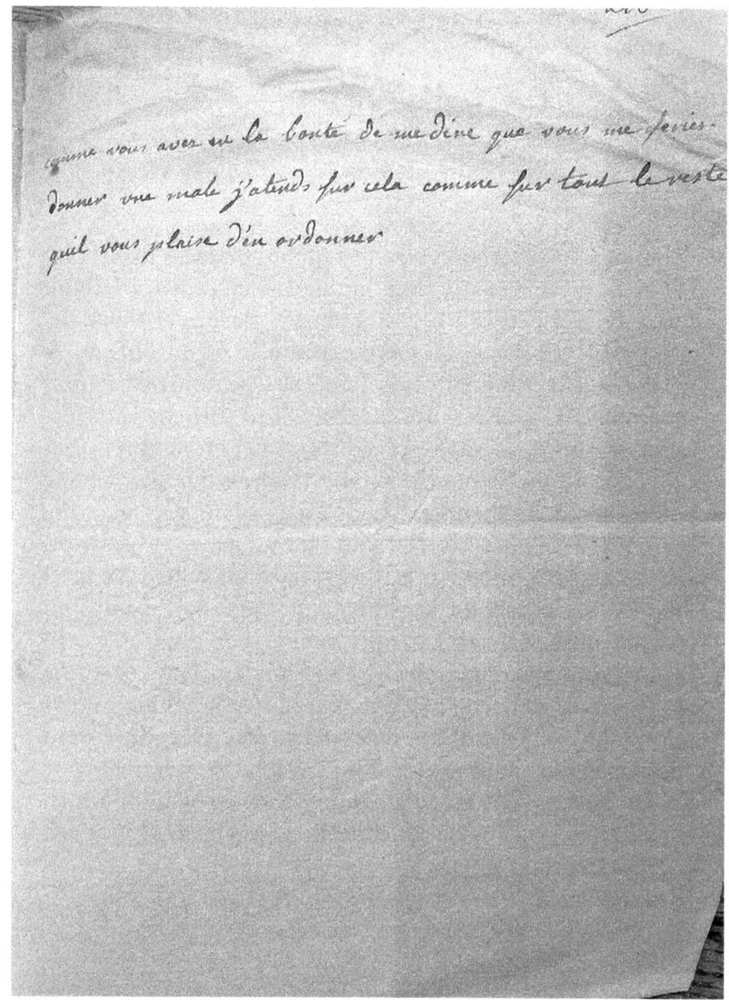

comme vous avez eu la bonté de me dire que vous me feriez
donner une male j'atends sur cela comme sur tout le reste
quil vous plaise d'en ordonner

Figure 3.6 Page three of letter from Bonafon to the Monseigneur. Photograph by the author.

Source: AB, MS 11582, 149.

grâces qui n'ajoutera pourtant rien à ma reconnaissance n'étant pas possible qu'elle augmente, je suis avec un très profond respect,

Monseigneur,

Votre très humble et très obéissante servant,

Bonafon.

[*Jointe au dossier de Mlle Bonafon, un bien guides du laisser passer la lettre qui est jointe à sa destination ce que j'ay retouché*]

Monseigneur the Major, having had the goodness to put give me back my old, used clothing, and your order is I think the only that actually keeps me in the Bastille, I think the delay that you bring to my departure is of an obligatory nature and it my weakness of the new season that ignites my problems, your pity for me truly filled with me with recognition and so many expressions (terms) of goodness that I do not know which terms to use to express but after having made offered my humble thanks, I dare to notice that at the present the weather is softer and that we may not be forced to wait another month at least that my fault ruined the need for a quick remedy for it getting better and that there is no assured more efficient than my avoiding the rigor of the cold having nothing comparable to the boredom that consumes me, I put no importance on making haste and in consideration of my sadness of my state that you would truly wish to speed the moment of my freedom it will be an overarching of graces that would not add anything to my recognition which is no longer possible be added to because already I have the deepest respect (for you).

Monseigneur,

Your very humble and obedient servant,

Bonafon[46]

Ordre du roi:

Monsieur

Je joins icy l'ordre du roi pour faire sortir du couvent des Bernardines de Moulins La dlle Bonafon, La mte (mentionnée) veux bien lui conservée trois cents livres par un pour la subsistance vous voulez bien l'en avertir ; il faudra aussi que je sois informe du jour qu'elle sortira du couvent de moulin afin

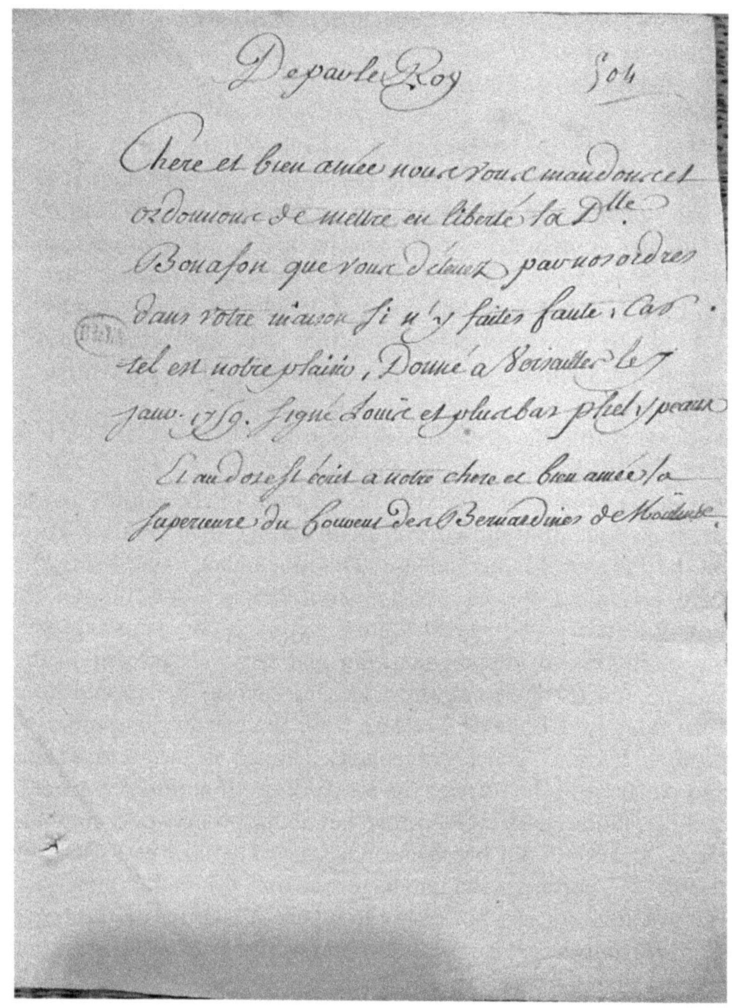
De par le Roy 504

Chere et bien amée nous vous mandons et
ordonnons de mettre en liberté la D^lle.
Bonafon que vous detenez par nos ordres
dans votre maison si n'y faites faute, car
tel est notre plaisir, Donné a Versailles le 7
janv. 1759. signé Louis et plus bas phelypeaux

Et au dos est écrit a notre chere et bien amée la
superieure du couvent des Bernardines de Moulins.

Figure 3.7 The *placet*. Photograph by the author.

Source: AB, MS 11582, 504.

que je fasse l'expédier l'ordonnance pour ce qui se trouvera ou de sa pension. Je suis toujours et très parfaitement. Votre très humble est très affine serviteur,

Morriesseszl M. Bertin

Sir,

I attach here the order of the king to enable Mlle de Bonafon to leave the convent of the Bernardines of Moulins. The aforementioned will receive three hundred pounds a year for her subsistence, would you be so kind and to inform her; it is also necessary that I be informed of the day that she is released from the convent of Moulin so that I may expedite the ordonnance and that she may receive her pension. I remain your perfectly humble and very attentive servant…

M. Bertin [the new Chief of Police].[47]

The legal brief that contains the records of Bonafon's arrest, interrogation, and subsequent legal actions also holds a copy of the "*placet*" for her release. This document, comprising the legal command for her release from the convent, illuminates Bonafon's story and provides greater context. We have explored her intentions to impugn the king and her consignment to the Bastille and then the convent. A crime such as hers could have been fatal, and Bonafon's release from the convent is significant proof of her intelligence and tenacity. Though she was refused pen and paper from the start of the proceedings, Bonafon persevered, and her handwritten letters prove her ability to network, communicate, and eventually overcome. She learned to liaise with the right people; she perfected the language and tone for each interaction. Her writings suggest not only the rebellious nature of the novel *Tanastès*, but they also reveal Bonafon's strategy of self-protection and her plan for survival.

The novel *Tanastès* provides a glimpse of the true workings of the royal court. Though it was fantasy, it focused on the dynamics of the court in a way not previously captured. She showed the king in all his sexual weakness. Louis XV concentrated on creating a powerful image of himself, much of which was dependent on his sexual potency. His conquests were famous, and this is a fact of which he was very proud. His lovers, especially his favorites, enjoyed royal privilege and, like the Marquise de Pompadour, became some of the most influential women in Europe. Mlle de Bonafon dared to write against the king and his mistress and survived the punishment for her crime.

The novel work of Bonafon can be seen through a different feminist lens, and rather than being critics of her style, we can appreciate her courage in challenging the court. She also demonstrated mastery of the belletristic form through her tenacious and well-thought-out strategy, written and communicated from confinement. We might well seek to appreciate that the body of Bonafon's writing is considerable in volume and its scope serves as a testament to her intelligence and her successful strategy of regaining a good deal of agency over her life. The case of Mlle Bonafon is also particularly interesting in the realm of forensic interpretations. Bonafon's style, spelling, and penmanship all suggest that she was well practiced above her station as chambermaid. Her work, the roman-à-clef, and the letters composed from prison and convent, have proven a rich subject for literary study. The legal brief in its entirety, and not only her roman-à-clef and its key, holds the possibility of expanding our understanding of the literature of the time, but especially the literature produced by women. In this exploration of the work of Bonafon, we should consider not only her novels but also the writings surrounding her arrest and consignment. Bonafon's extant material within her factum, the body of forensic or evidentiary materials, together with her letters, including her expressions of contrition and justifications of her actions, help us to understand more deeply the role of women in a particular milieu of the period. The literature is especially compelling, forcing one to consider what it must have been like to reach for pen and paper, illicitly obtained, and to plead for one's reputation and life under the most difficult of circumstances.

Notes

1 One last point to consider in the passage from political to literary character entails the intimacy and individualization associated with reading in the eighteenth century. We can assume that these novels were read aloud in small groups and by individuals in the comfort of salons, studies, and reading rooms. In either case, however, the gesture differs from the crowd gathered to watch the king eat dinner or enter a city. These small volumes resembled a miniature portrait that readers could contemplate and appropriate in personal and

diverse ways. Readers cultivated self-awareness as they engaged with these texts and developed responses to them. The didactic energy of fiction compelled readers to improve themselves and their society by learning from the examples they encountered. In addition, these novels targeted Louis XV himself, explicitly or implicitly, with their tales of error and redemption. Yet, if the king failed to mend his ways, the novels summoned readers to resist abuse and neglect through the supporting characters who exemplified principles of moral courage and enlightened ideology.

2 For an in-depth discussion of this notion, see Robert Darnton, *The Forbidden Best-Sellers of Pre-Revolutionary France* (W.W. Norton, 1996), 378.

3 Historical and scholarly interest in *Tanastès* is largely due to Robert Darnton's article "Mademoiselle Bonafon and the Private Life of Louis XV: Communication Circuits in Eighteenth-Century France," *Représentations* 87, no. 1 (2004): 102-124, and to Lisa Jane Graham's work in a separate study, "Fiction, Kingship and the Politics of Character in Eighteenth-Century France," in *Mystifying the Monarch: Studies on Discourse, Power, and History*, ed. Jeroen Deploige and Gita Deneckere (Amsterdam: Amsterdam University Press, 2006), 139-58. Both historians examine Bonafon's file in depth and contextualize Bonafon's novel and reception within the study of the diffusion of French eighteenth-century court gossip. Though they have examined it in depth, the story surrounding the text still has great implications for women's studies in general, in that the defiant act of one woman could have seriously damaged the crown's reputation.

4 The only proof we have of these plays is the actual testimony of Bonafon, in the court file in Paris, Archives de la Bastille (AB), MS 115872, 118-20. The idea they may have included illicit content is not farfetched. The presence of these plays also sparks the question: Was *Tanastès* destined for the stage as was many a roman-à-clef?

5 For a full explanation of the legal role of the *Lettres de Cachet* see Arlette Farge, *Dire et mal dire. L'opinion publique au XVIIIe siècle* (Paris: Editions du Seuil, 1992), 165.

6 "The intended prohibition was seemingly on the production of letters but could also have been the kings' fear she may produce yet more clandestine literature." Darnton, "Mademoiselle Bonafon," 114.

7 Ibid.

8 Most of the files, unless otherwise noted, come from case file AB, MS 11582.

9 It is of note that the Princesse de Mauntaubon was linked to the "parti devôt."

10 Darnton, "Mademoiselle Bonafon," 104.

11 Direct mention of this appears in the case file AB, MS 11582, 143-142.

12 Ibid., 118.

13 As Darnton suggests, "Deciphering keys was a literary game for an elite trained to decode political culture based on secrecy, conspiracy and allusion." "Mademoiselle Bonafon," 108-109.

14 "The combination of good and bad qualities made Tanastès a credible and complex literary character. Yet, by revealing the king's flaws and inconsistencies, Bonafon dispelled the mystique attached to his person." Graham, "Fiction, Kingship," 148.

15 Bonafon recalled Richelieu's notion of exemplary behavior to chide the selfish Agamil. The reference to a king who abandoned his duty for sexual dalliance struck a chord among French readers concerned about Louis XV's capacity to lead them in a time of war. Bonafon used interior monologue to flesh out Agamil's character and to collapse the distance separating the king from the reader. For example, after his marriage to Sterlie, Agamil wrestles with his pledge of conjugal fidelity but refuses to give up his mistress. He justifies his behavior by reminding himself that *"un roi n'est pas fait pour être victime des loix qu'il impose aux autres.*" Translation: "A King is not made to be a victim of the law that he imposes on others." All translation and transcription by the author unless otherwise stated.

16 Bonafon adds why she chose to represent such an "interesting" character to her testimony. "*Ce caractère ambigu, mêlé de bien et de mal était alors à la mode; ainsi après bien des agitations, il en fut quitte pour se mettre au niveau des hommes ordinaires.*" Translation: "This ambiguous character mixed with good and bad was very in fashion and with some molding it was necessary to put [him] at the level of ordinary men." AB, MS 11582, 155.

17 Darnton, "Mademoiselle Bonafon," 108.

18 Here I begin to take issue with my colleagues and wish to refer from now on to Bonafon simply as author.

19 "Mlle Bonafon may not have been a great writer, but she occupied a critical position where oral and written versions of events converged. From this point onward, the process gained momentum. 'Mauvais propos' and books poured out, carrying a negative account of the monarchy to increasingly broad sectors of the public. It was the famous deluge, which began in the middle of Louis XV's reign, not afterward, and it had a crucial effect on the view of contemporary history." Darnton, "Mademoiselle Bonafon," 114.

20 Darnton, "Mademoiselle Bonafon," 115.

21 Ibid., 105. This comment is about AB, MS 11582, 104.

22 Janet Altman confirms this notion: "The literacy of convent women enabled them to appeal to authorities outside their convents on

numerous occasions, long before Diderot wrote *La Religieuse*." "Women's Letters in the Public Sphere," in *Going Public: Women and Publishing in Early Modern Times*, eds. Elizabeth Goldsmith and Dena Goodman (Ithaca: Cornell University Press, 1995), 109.

23 "The handwriting in the files reflects that she drafted the play *Tanastès* herself, and that the letters in the brief were also written in her hand. She had confessed to having written two plays and two novels. Fiction required narrative techniques to uncover the emotions and communicate them to readers." Graham, "Fiction, Kingship," 140.

24 Dena Goodman speaks to the fact that even women who were literate were very likely to not have an education equal to that of men, which included instruction in Latin. See *Becoming a Woman in the Age of Letters* (Ithaca: Cornell University Press, 2009), 63-157.

25 AB, MS 11582, 64.

26 While Darnton repeatedly speaks of the low quality of the writing of Bonafon's work and explains that the second half is too convoluted to even use in his precis. Ibid., 114, footnote 14.

27 Graham argues that form in the novel plays a determining role in this type of literature: "Too much attention has focused on the content of texts, images, and utterances and not enough on modes and mechanisms of communication. To counter this tendency, I have turned to Michel de Certeau, who warns against the ideology of 'consumption-as-a-receptacle.'" "Fiction, Kingship," 147.

28 "Previous descriptions of despotism had always distanced the threat in time and place, but Bonafon puts the reference inside the mind of the royal character." Ibid., 142.

29 AB, MS 11582, 118.

30 Graham, 148.

31 It is interesting how many short novellas became plays, and this had greater potential for damage to the court. Graham says of this phenomenon: "In contrast to political propaganda and royal ceremonies, these novels were not commissioned and controlled by the crown. Louis XV lost control of his character in this decade, neither he, nor his successor managed to reclaim it." "Fiction, Kingship," 141-142.

32 Darnton's focus is on how this story was communicated to the public: "A chambermaid in Versailles was shut up in the Bastille for publishing a roman-à-clef about the sex life of Louis XV. In attempting to get to the bottom of the case, the police uncovered a remarkable amount of information about how oral media and print culture interested." "Mademoiselle Bonafon," 102.

33 Janet Altman, *Epistolarity: Approaches to a Form* (Columbus: Ohio State University Press, 1982), 118.

34 AB, MS 11582, 261

35 Goodman, *Becoming a Woman*, 60.

36 AB, MS 11582, 144-145.

37 It could well be that because Princess Montauban was linked to the "parti devôt" and therefore threatened by the power of Richelieu and the king's mistresses.

38 Ibid., 147.

39 Nancy Miller, *The Poetics of Gender* (New York: Columbia University Press, 1986), xiii.

40 "Of course, prison archives have a built-in bias: they concern persons deemed to be criminal; so they can give the misleading impression that everyone was bad-mouthing the government. But the police also compiled reports on what ordinary people said in cafes, public gardens, and marketplaces. A network of spies perhaps as many as three thousand-provided the information, and primitive journalists, like the notorious chevalier de Mouhy, wrote it up in bulletins furnished every day to the lieutenant general, who then adapted it for presentation to the minister for the department of Paris and, eventually, the king. In short, the police produced a gazette of their own. Copies were leaked, for a price, to important grandees, like the marechal de Saxe, one of Mouhy's clandestine customers. And several copies survive, though only in fragments, in various archives; so we can begin to put together an account of the public noises picked up by the police. It is a tricky business, because the police gazeteers filtered their information and wrote it up in ways that would ingratiate themselves with their superiors. One cannot read them literally." Darnton, "Mademoiselle Bonafon," 111.

41 Ibid.

42 The language seems to have evolved after her transfer, as compared to Gravelle's writing, which devolved once she was in the convent.

43 "In fact, Mlle Bonafon remained in the Bastille for fourteen and a half months. Her health deteriorated so badly that, according to a report from the Bastille's governor, she seemed likely to die unless she were transferred to a healthier site. She was therefore shut up in the convent of the Bernardines at Moulins, where she remained, without permission to receive either visitors or letters for the next twelve years." Darnton, "Mademoiselle Bonafon," 108.

44 "As an author, Bonafon had options for manipulating characters and resolving problems that real life denied to ministers and princes. The police reports confirm that Bonafon's fiction encouraged readers to draw conclusions deemed to be "insulting" to the king and his authority." Graham, "Fiction, Kingship," 148.

45 AB, MS 11582, 218.

46 Ibid., 209. Attached to this dossier of Mlle Bonafon, is a note to let this letter which I have edited and modified reach its destination.

47 Ibid., 266.

References

Altman, Janet. “Women’s Letters in the Public Sphere.” In *Going Public: Women and Publishing in Early Modern Times*. Edited by Elizabeth C. Goldsmith and Dena Goodman, 99–115. Ithaca: Cornell University Press, 1995.

Altman, Janet. *Epistolarity: Approaches to a Form*. Columbus: Ohio State University Press, 1982.

Darnton, Robert. “Mademoiselle Bonafon and the Private Life of Louis XV: Communication Circuits in Eighteenth-Century France.” *Représentations* 87, no. 1 (2004): 102–124.

Darnton, Robert. *The Forbidden Best-Sellers of Pre-Revolutionary France*. W.W. Norton, 1996.

Farge, Arlette. *Dire et mal dire: L’opinion publique au XVIIIe siècle*. Paris: Le Seuil, 1992.

Graham, Lisa Jane. “Fiction, Kingship and the Politics of Character in Eighteenth-Century France.” In *Mystifying the Monarch: Studies on Discourse, Power, and History*, edited by Jeroen Deploige and Gita Deneckere, 139–58. Amsterdam: Amsterdam University Press, 2006.

Goldsmith, Elizabeth C. and Dena Goodman. “Introduction.” In *Going Public: Women and Publishing in Early Modern Times*. Edited by Elizabeth C. Goldsmith and Dena Goodman, 1–10. Ithaca: Cornell University Press, 1995.

Goodman, Dena. *Becoming a Women in the Age of Letters*. Ithaca: Cornell University Press, 2009.

Miller, Nancy. *The Poetics of Gender*. New York: Columbia University Press, 1986.

4 Excess or Success?

The Case of Mme Geneviève de Gravelle

Geneviève de Gravelle's correspondence—that is, her awkward and ungrammatical excess of words—challenged the king's sovereignty solely by existing. Her letters and notes were chaotic and at times unclear, yet Gravelle herself can be understood contextually through the efforts she made to be heard by the public. Her challenge to kingly sovereignty came through as much in her epistolary excess as in the sound arguments she marshaled against her own marginalization. Exploring the barriers Gravelle faced in writing and in being read, as well as her varied efforts to overcome those barriers, sheds light on the closed attitudes held by the court towards women, and more specifically unmarried and middle-aged women. Sometimes her letters revealed a strategic or self-reflexive awareness of their own rhetorical tactics. These letters are preserved in the Bastille Archives dating from 1745 to 1751 and they address questions of contemporary women's lives and actions.[1] We can support our understanding of the letters by referring to the other contents of her file. Taking note of the objects, lists, and order forms adds to the narrative that has to date been only incompletely conveyed about this woman. I seek to employ a more expansive and modern approach, as we have recourse to the approaches of modern literary theorists and historians for considering women's agency in eighteenth-century France.

Geneviève de Gravelle was an unmarried woman who would have been subject to the negative judgment of her time regarding her marital status, expressed by the French address "*mademoiselle*," which roughly translates to the outdated English term "spinster."

DOI: 10.4324/9780429001147-5

She was, in most respects, a product of her class and steeped in the principles of a noble upbringing. She spent much of her early life, so far as we can discern, voluntarily residing in different convents to engage in spiritual reflection and respite from life in society. She was closely related to members of the court, and during one of her stays in the convent she met and became close with Mademoiselle de Béthune, an impoverished noblewoman. Gravelle was instrumental in arranging a match for Béthune to a man of significant standing, Pâris de Monmartel, who served as financier to King Louis XV. Béthune's marriage was regarded as a great success by the king and the court, and as recompense Gravelle repeatedly asked Monmartel for a pension to help her maintain her lifestyle when living outside the convent. The negative response from the Monmartels was swift and definitive, but Gravelle refused to take *non* for an answer![2]

She repeated her requests, arguing that it was only right to be compensated for her role in making such an advantageous match.[3] Perhaps out of embarrassment, or wanting to punish her for the audacity of her request, the Monmartels arranged for a series of *lettres de cachet* against Gravelle to be drawn up with the approval and imprimatur of the king, duly signed by his minister.[4]

We know of this not only because some of the *lettres de cachet* are preserved in Gravelle's file, but also due to the well-known and highly-connected Cardinal Joly de Fleury's letter to police secretary Duval, inquiring about the whereabouts of the royal letter and about Gravelle herself.

> *Je vous prie, Monsieur de vouloir bien me mander si vous avez eu connaissance d'un ordre du Roy donne au mois de décembre de l'année dernière, en vertu duquel de la Dlle Geneviève Gravelle a été conduitte a la maison des filles Pénitentes de la ville d'Angers ou elle est encore : en ce cas, vous me feriez plaisir de m'instruire des motifs qui ont donné lieu à cet ordre. On ne peut être avec un plus sincère ny plus inviolable attachement que je le suis, Monsieur,*
> *Votre très humble et très obéissant serviteur,*
> *Joly de Fleury*
>
> Please Monsieur, I beseech you to tell me if you have any knowledge of an order (a citation) from the king given in December last year, in the name of the virtuous Mademoiselle Geneviève de Gravelle who was taken to the "Convent of the Penitent Girls" in the town of Angers where she should

> still reside today; if this is the case, would you do me the pleasure of communicating the motives that have given rise to this order. One couldn't be more sincere or have a stronger connection than that of myself, Monsieur,
>
> Your very humble and very obedient servant,
>
> Joly de Fleury[5]

The king's self-consciousness and vulnerability are reflected in his agreement to write the first *lettre de cachet*. From the early stages of Gravelle's letter writing, the king had ordered her (as with other cases in this book) to cease her entreaties.[6] He then wrote an order to deprive her of access to pen and paper. However, the king's instructions were evidently not followed, and his instructions did not bring an end to her unraveled and prolific discourse. Before doing so, the king performed his due diligence by way of his relationship with Joly de Fleury. Fleury was most obviously asked to consult with the king on this most embarrassing of situations; he was a great protector of the reputation of the king, but he was concerned about the reputation of the court overall as well. He was a preceptor and counselor to Louis XV at the time of Gravelle's imprisonment, and here he shows his obvious concern with how the developing "noise" surrounding Gravelle would appear to the public (Figures 4.1–4.2).[7]

Gravelle was confined to the Paris monastery of Madeleine-de-la-Flèche by a *lettre de cachet* in March 1748, which conveyed orders directly to its addressee. The first *lettre de cachet* was issued at the request of Pâris de Monmartel. Gravelle had played a role in negotiating Monmartel's 1746 marriage to the impoverished noblewoman. Mademoiselle de Béthune had enough of Gravelle's demands for recompense for her matchmaking services. Gravelle had become an embarrassment if not a liability to the couple.

Wingrove has determined the timeline of Gravelle's ordered removal from court life, her cloistering, and her removal to prison:

> Almost immediately after being detained, Gravelle began writing letters decrying the injustice of her situation. Passed by hand and deposited at the post by sympathetic or bribed residents of the monastery, her narratives of aristocratic abuse and the disregard for her 'good right' began circulating in Paris. The monastery officials in charge of Gravelle's care requested and received an order prohibiting her from all writing. But the

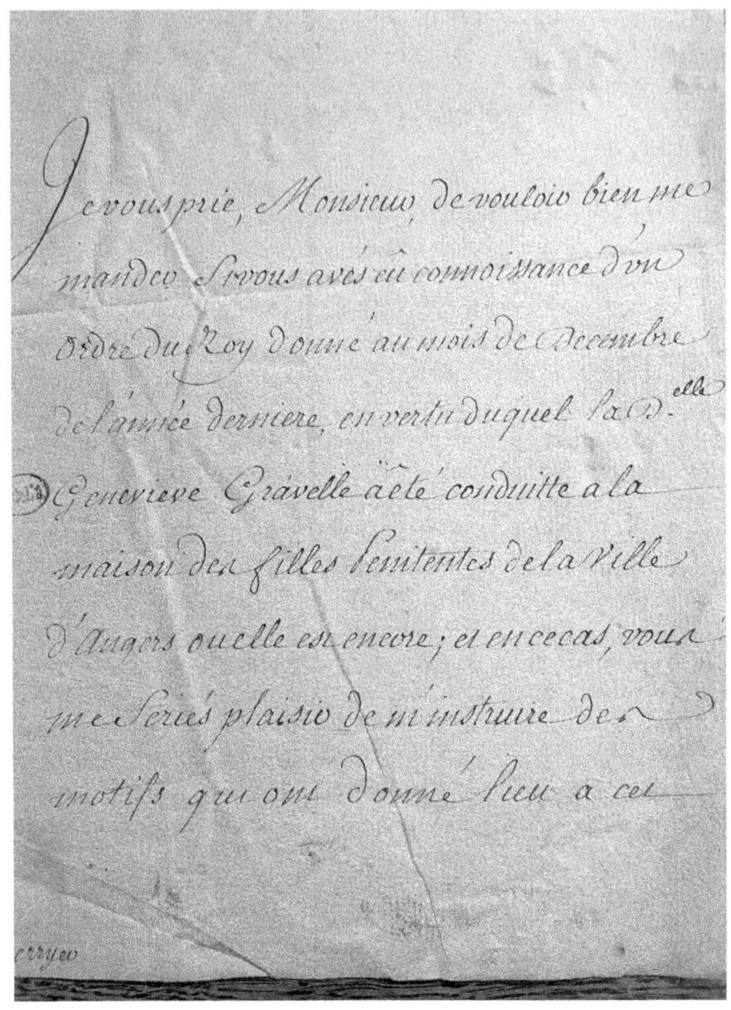

Je vous prie, Monsieur, de vouloir bien me
mander si vous avés eu connoissance d'un
ordre du Roy donné au mois de Decembre
de l'année derniere, en vertu duquel la D.lle
Genevieve Gravelle a été conduitte a la
maison des filles Penitentes de la ville
d'Angers ou elle est encore; et en ce cas, vous
me seriés plaisir de m'instruire des
motifs qui ont donné lieu a cet

Figure 4.1 Page one of letter from Cardinal Joly de Fleury to Duval. Photograph by the author.

Source: Wingrove, "Sovereign Address," 142.

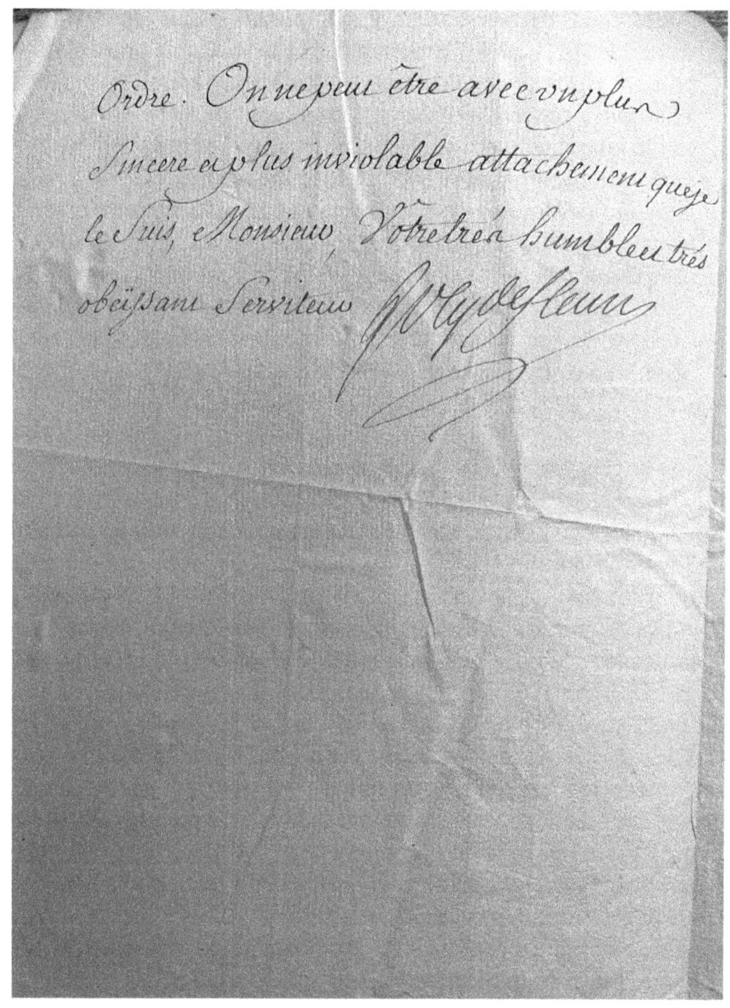

Ordre. On ne peut être avec un plus
sincere et plus inviolable attachement que je
le suis, Monsieur, Votre trés humble et trés
obeïssant Serviteur Joly de Fleury

Figure 4.2 Page two of letter from Cardinal Joly de Fleury to Duval. Photograph by the author.

Source: Wingrove, "Sovereign Address," 142.

> missives continued to appear. An exasperated Monmartel sent police chief Berryer letters of complaint, which resulted in a second *lettre de cachet* ordering her transfer to the more closely policed Hôpital des Penitents outside the capital in Angers. That move proved ineffective. Letters and *mémoires* addressed to the king, members of the nobility, and presidents of various *parlements* continued to surface over the next two years; a *third lettre de cachet* was requested and issued, this time ordering her transfer to the Bastille. Gravelle's confinement in the château reserved for political prisoners seems to have brought an end to her epistolary output; records indicate that a fourth *lettre de cachet* ordering her transfer to Vincennes two years later was prompted by overcrowding at the Bastille.[8]

The legal brief of Geneviève de Gravelle is voluminous, and this is largely because of her prolific epistolary production. Was this case file an example of political writing? No one at the time would have classified it as such, due to its messy nature and all-too-improvisational nature. Was her chaotic and long-winded writing an example of a certain literary "style" that produces a "poetics of gender?"[9] Often women's epistolary writing of the time is associated with feeling, while men's written output is connected to reason. Dena Goodman asserts that this is reflective of the different kinds of education they received.[10]

Overall, her writing bordered on a kind of graphomania and might lead readers today (and in her own time) to wonder if she was of sound mind. Yet here we investigate what role this extensive writing played in her life of confinement. Did she truly expect her letters to reach a powerful and sympathetic reader, and to bear fruit and eventually procure her freedom?[11] Could she have reasonably anticipated replies or any response to her missives? As we will see, her communication lacked self-consciousness (certainly in comparison to the other case files presented in this book). We can, however, view her letters as a kind of self-empowerment, or even a strategy to overwhelm the king and demonstrate the need for his mercy and clemency. They most likely had a therapeutic effect on Gravelle herself. Gravelle's letters reflected an immediacy of speech and demonstrated more than the formality of studied expression or artistic convention. This is how Gravelle mediated the issue of voice and agency. The written sense of her letters was at times precarious, and her messages often appear scrambled, but

Gravelle's need to be seen and heard is clear. She used all she could to be as "visible" and "heard" as possible.

The dossier treated in this chapter (Figure 4.3) is over 420 pages long and fills a whole file box, while most of the files at the library

Figure 4.3 Gravelle's legal dossier. Photograph by the author.

Source: AB, MS 11769.

are only a few pages. Naturalness was exaggerated in Gravelle's writing due to its spontaneity and improvisational manner. French women's letter writing (especially in responses to authority) usually contained some stiltedness because of the formulaic addresses of politeness to which they were forced to adhere. But conversely there was much more freedom in written expression for them than for their male counterparts once the pleasantries were expressed. As Goodman remarks in her work on women's epistolarity in eighteenth-century France, "Letter writing fell somewhere between speech and reflective writing. Defined as conversation with someone who is absent, it was ordinary language simply laced on a page; it was writing in the way one speaks."[12] In principle, letter writing anticipated a response and is often one half of the "dialogic style." The letter itself could be obtuse and the testimonial style reflective of larger issues, for example those of abuse, neglect, and calculated disempowerment.

Examining writing practices while considering the issue of authorial intention is perplexing. Gravelle had been criticized by the king, the nobles at court, and her mother superior for writing and sending an abundance of poorly written letters. We are led to question why Gravelle would open herself up to such criticism. If Gravelle indeed intended to ingratiate herself with the king and receive a pension, why would she harass him in such a way? In her more legible and coherent letters, it seems there may have been a level of conscious sacrifice in her approach. Gravelle was made a victim, further marginalized both physically and emotionally by the court after early attempts to be recognized for her efforts (and by recognition, we mean *reimbursement*). One implication of her actions is that she was speaking to the experience of powerlessness specifically because she was a woman. There is a significant incongruence between her aristocratic status and her lack of agency. She attested consistently to the unfairness of this fact.[13]

Gravelle's dossier includes many long-winded, scribbled letters and copies of letters that were written to her. It includes the *lettres de cachet,* many replies, task-oriented lists, and even orders placed by Gravelle herself for essential items such as clothing and curtains.[14] Apparently Gravelle had a system for writing and disseminating her letters long before she was imprisoned. She seems to have been a natural at networking, and so she utilized her social networks when under attack. As the oppression increased, so did her letter writing (and copying) and means of epistolary dissemination. As Elizabeth Wingrove has shown, "Passed by hand and deposited at the post by sympathetic or bribed residents of the monastery, her narratives of aristocratic abuse and the disregard for her 'good right' began circulating in Paris."[15] Wingrove's earlier work on the difficulty of reading Gravelle's letters due to their extraordinary "*ampleur*" sheds light on Gravelle's situation but falls short of examining possibilities for further interpretation.[16]

Though difficult, reading Gravelle's file does provide a measure of insight into her personal and emotional struggles and the context and history of her life. The ambiguity of her writing paradoxically leads to a certain clarity about her situation. One cannot help but empathize with her panic and fury over her treatment. We should not simply dismiss her as insane or irrational, as she was likely regarded by her jailers and oppressors. Gravelle found ways to send her missives, and they were indeed circulated in salons and cafés, and gossip spread as a result. Somehow (the records are mute regarding the details), Gravelle was supplied with pen and paper and continued to write.

After a brief stay in the convent, Gravelle was moved to a workhouse as punishment for her writing. These workhouses were convent-style institutions that included a work component and were often used as punishment for unruly women.[17] After reading the letters from the reigning Mother Superior, Monsallier, one might speculate that she thought it could therapeutically console Gravelle to write letters and thus stop her from agitating within the convent walls. However, we can see in the letters issued by the Mother Superior that she grew increasingly frustrated with Gravelle's behavior over time (as seen in Figure 4.10). Gravelle accused the highest authorities of abuses of power. She was then transferred from the convent of Madeleine-de-la Flèche to the workhouse at L'Hôpital d'Angers by *lettre de cachet* (order of the king). The letter below describes the transfer. Letters from the Mother Superior continued as she reported on Gravelle from the convent and told the king of Gravelle's uncontrollable behavior.

The letter figured above (Figure 4.3) is the first preserved copy of a full letter in her dossier, of which she herself sent multiple copies, and demonstrates how Gravelle began to execute her plan of "attack by overflow."[18] There may have been a dual purpose. Gravelle could have copied letters she had received to keep track of them; but wouldn't one copy of a letter have been sufficient? Her constant copying apparently had an effect as her letters circulated through the usual gossip circuits. It seems she had clients for whom she was a professional go-between, arranging furniture sales and employment connections, in addition to spousal introductions. Here is one such letter, attribution unknown.

> *[Copies de letter] À Mlle de Gravelle chez Monsieur Gauttier, rue des chausseurs proche du Louvre à Paris, de…le 7 février 1745*
>
> *Je ne dois cesser de vous adresser des remercîments ma chère Mademoiselle puisque vos témoignages d'amitié pour moi sont continuelle j'ay trouver en Madame votre sœur la meilleure sorte de femme qu'on puisse voir attentive à ce c'est bonne le cœur prévenant et bien faisant elle est toute aimables à connaitre ses…*
>
> [Copy of letter] To Mlle de Gravelle, chez M. Gautier, rue de chausseurs near the Louvre in Paris, de…7 February 1745
>
> I cannot stop thanking you my dear Mademoiselle, your demonstrations of friendship to me continue and I have found in Madame, your sister, the best kind of woman that one could see; she is attentive and of good and well-meaning heart makes her most lovable to all who know her…[19]

There is no escaping the impression that her corpus of letters is chaotic, and so one must adopt a certain methodology to read them. There are letters addressed to Gravelle that she copied herself. The above letter and its address (Figure 4.4) are examples of Gravelle's habit of copying letters that were written to her, and doing so several times, in fact. Gravelle's copied letters were sent and resent. This speaks to the level of "noise" she was trying to create. Through her overwhelming epistolary production, Gravelle's suffering becomes visible and therefore more intelligible. The struggles she spoke of (when legible) reflected several issues that scholars of eighteenth-century feminist history report as the norm rather than the exception.[20] Her feelings of being unheard, disempowered, undervalued, and muzzled by the king and the aristocracy are all highlighted in these letters. The injustice she experienced was mediated through her written and textual voice. Part of what allows us to consider this writing as being contextually gendered female is the vivid sense

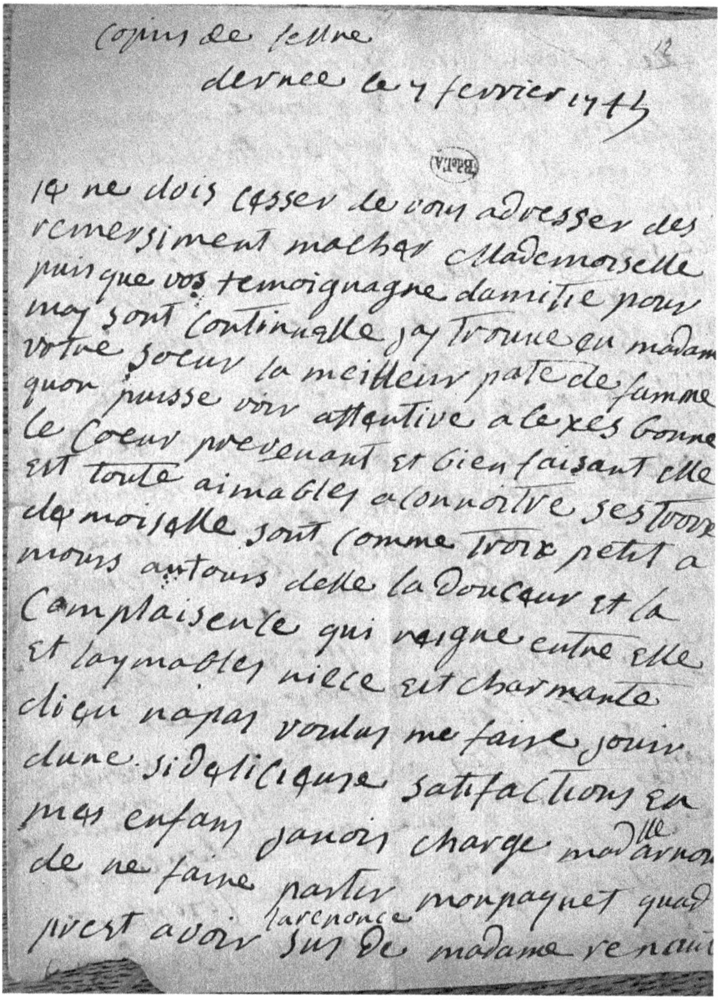

Copies de lettre
devnee le 7 fevrier 1745

je ne dois cesser de vous adresser des
remersiment malhar Mademoiselle
puisque vos temoignagne damitie pour
moy sont Continualle jay trouve en madam
votre soeur la meilleur pate de famme
quon puisse voir attentive a le xes Bonne
le Coeur prevenant et bien faisant elle
est toute aimables a connoitre ses trois
demoisalle sont comme trois petit a
mours autours delle la douceur et la
Complaisente qui raigne entre elle
et laymables niece est charmante
dieu napas voulus me faire jouir
dune si delicicquse satifactions en
mes enfans javois charge mdlle arnou
de ne faire partir monpaquet quap
pres avoir larenonce sus de madame renau

Figure 4.4 Page one of letter received from an unknown acquaintance and copied by Gravelle. Photograph by the author.

Source: AB, MS 11769, 12.

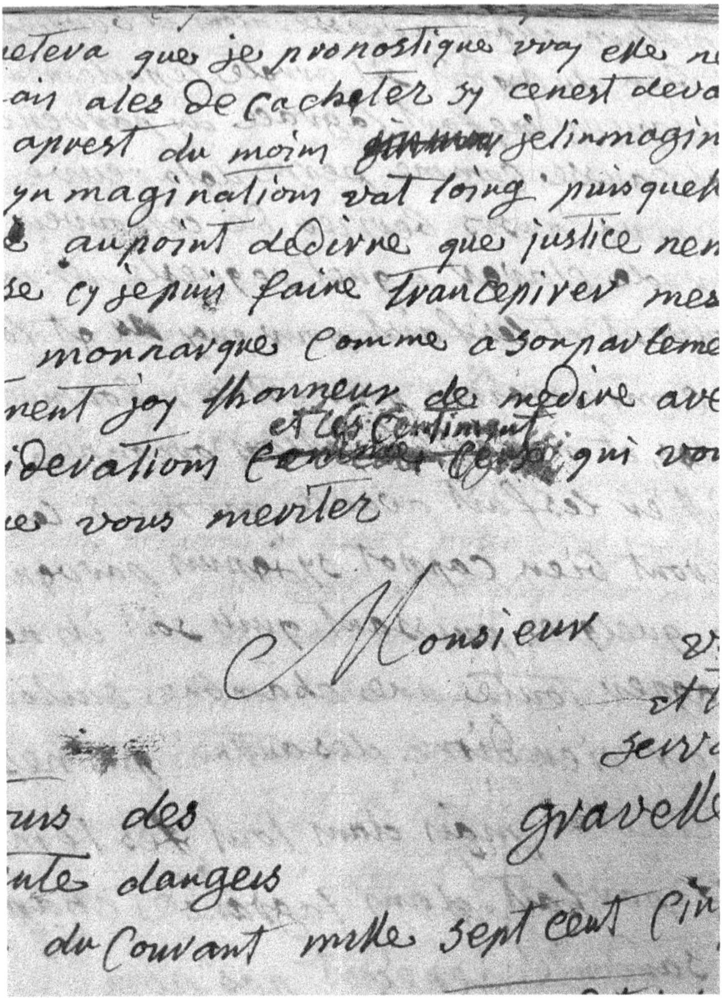
etera que je pronostique vray elle n
ais ales decacheter sy cenest deva
aprest du moins ~~[illegible]~~ jelinmagin
yn magination vat loing puisque
au point dedivre que justice nen
se cy je puis faire trancepirer mes
monrarque comme a son parleme
nent jay lhonneur de me dire ave
et les sentiment
idevations ~~[illegible]~~ qui vo
es vous meriter

Monsieur
et
serv
us des
gravelle
nte dangers
du Courant mille sept cent cin

Figure 4.5 Page two of letter received from an unknown acquaintance and copied by Gravelle. Photograph by the author.

Source: AB, MS 11769, 12.

of vulnerability that we can sense in Gravelle's writing. While men might have used the expression of vulnerability for exploitative purposes as well, there appears to have been nothing calculated or insincere in Gravelle's expression.

While as readers we typically search for narrative coherence, in this instance we would do well to stand back from the text and appreciate the reality of its expression. This file reflects a chaotic thought process, and often the reading process feels like swimming in the rapid waters of someone's stream of consciousness. There is a frustrated personal voice and a politically gendered tonality throughout these letters. Especially when addressing Madame de Montmartel, Gravelle tried to catch her attention and direct comments to her, woman to woman. Though indeed, greater legibility would grant greater access, assembling the fragments can help us understand Gravelle's story cohesively as an experience of the loss of agency. The paradox is that the more she unraveled in her letters, the more her story comes together as a whole.

Using historical, contextual, and literary tools, one can discern a pattern of distress. It is most significant to observe Gravelle's devolution in style, language, and spirit. One notes her letters' proliferation of words, their repetition, and most of all their anger and sadness. In her writing's raw state, we see an authenticity of voice that is quite shocking. Wingrove underscores this point in her study of Gravelle:

> [T]he sensory challenges faced by proper *literary analysis* are multiple. The "blind and blinding speech" that confounds historiographers, for example, suggests words that lack and impair vision. Certainly, the phrase captures an aspect of the experience of reading Gravelle: the hundreds of pages of her letters weave in and out of legibility and grammaticality, while their materiality—smudged ink, to many pages, new prose written besides, around, and over old prose on the letters she sometimes used as stationary—strains and occasionally bewilders the reader.[21]

Let us take the issue of reader response theory as one way to read the unravelment of Gravelle's writing. Most of the letters in this file did not anticipate a response; rather, they demanded attention. These letters may be considered red flags of distress for Gravelle and perhaps other women in her situation. We have read about Bonafon's case in the previous chapter, and though more restrained, she found ways to write from the convent to avoid the king's censorship of her letters and to communicate her dismay over her ongoing situation. The therapeutic potential of these letters, or any letter writing for that matter, cannot be underestimated. There is a sense of perpetual need to be seen and heard in her letters, and she seems at the same time to be continuously venting at the world. The dates are clear on most of the documents, but the order of the file (like many of those in the Archives de la Bastille) is not chronological. The letters for this study of the trajectory of Gravelle's life of confinement begin in 1745, because that is the year Gravelle was in the convent with Béthune for a period of retreat. We see her transfer to the workhouse later in the letter from the Mother Superior of Monsallier and an account of her life in that period is recorded in a letter dated 19 January 1747.

Gravelle tried to reach out to the most well-connected people in the court in the hopes that they would put in a good word for her with the king. Amongst those well-connected nobles was the Duchesse de Lorge (Geneviève de Challimard) with whom she had a long-time friendship.

> *Gravelle a La Duchesse de Lorge dame d'honneur de son altesse Royale au Palais du roi*
>
> *A Paris*
>
> *Sans avoir l'honneur d'être connue de vous j'ay ce luy de m'adresser avec une parfaite confiance connaissant combien vous êtes remplis de contes à m'obliger née avec des qualifiées de cœur et d'esprit digne de votre naissance pouvay [pouvez] vous me refuse le plaisir de donner ce mémoire à son (h) altesse royale je me flatte Madame que vous ne refusez pas cette grâce à une Mme bien née qu'un malheur dont sans doute l'histoire n'a jamais entendu parler réduite dans une maison de force pour avoir "conçu" Mlle de Bethune de présenter de Monmartel d'une tendresse a toute et puisque vous verrez par ce mémoire cy joint cy j'ay raison de ne recevoir son justice madame la duchesse de…et duc de…m'eusse ont une bonne connaissance comme bien d'autre et par son aïeul a elle-même qu'elle tient de moy cet état bruyant…*

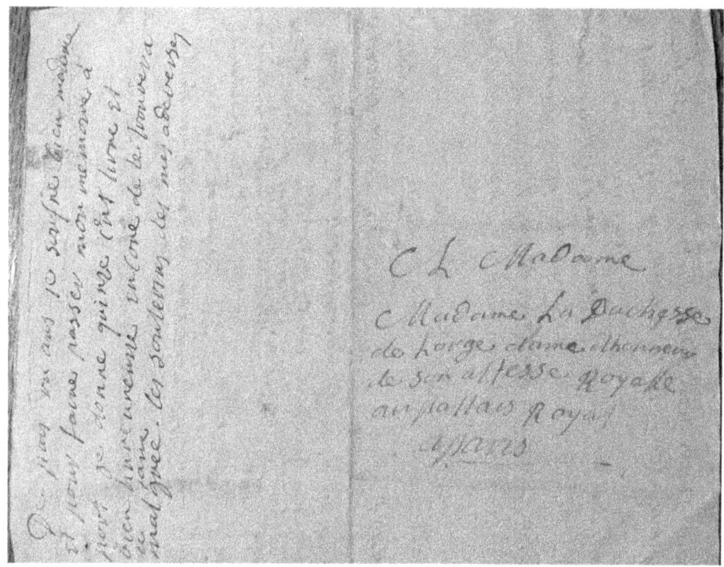

A Madame
Madame La Duchesse
de Lorge dame d'honneur
de son altesse Royalle
au pallais Royal
a paris

Figure 4.6 Page one of letter from Gravelle to the Duchess of Lorge. Photograph by the author.

Source: AB, MS 11769, 419.

> *...votre recommandation comblera mes vœux d'ayant en parler à sa majesté qui père plus que roi de son peuple m'accordera la levée de ma lettre de cachet.*

Gravelle to the Duchesse of Lorge, Lady of Honor of his Highness at the Palace of the King

Without having the honor of being known [introduced] to you, I feel that I can address you in perfect confidence knowing how you have already been filled in on the stories that obligate me, you are born with the qualities of heart and spirit dignified of your birth, you cannot refuse me the pleasure of giving this missive to his Royal Highness. I flatter myself, Madame that you would not refuse me the grace. To a well born woman who has suffered an unhappy story of which you most certainly not heard that I have been reduced to a live in a workhouse after having conceived to introduce

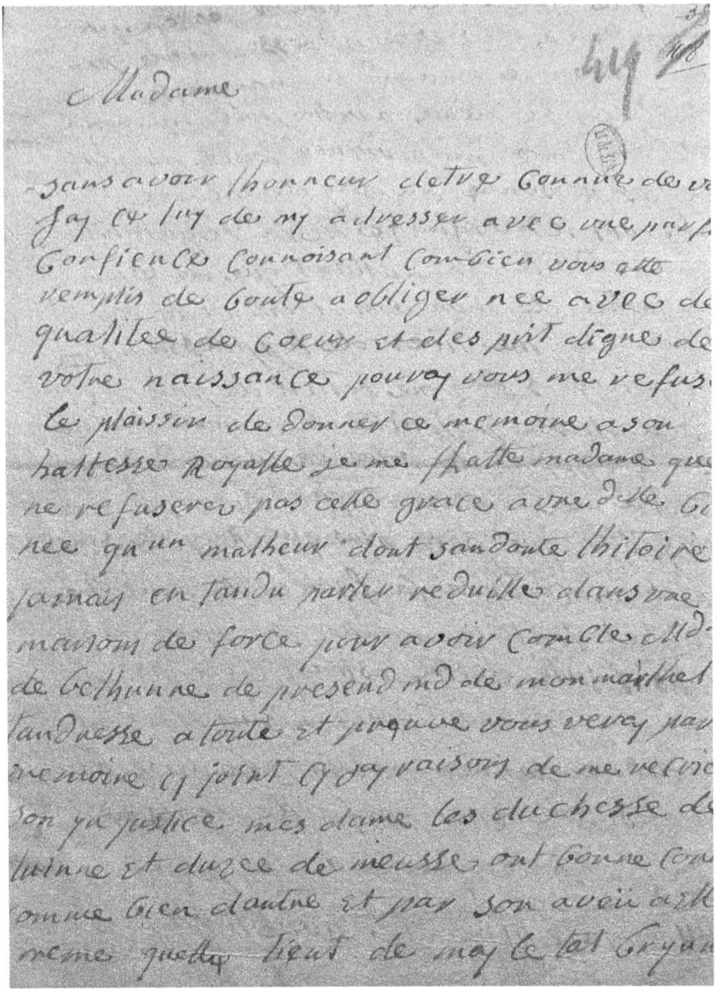

Madame

sans avoir lhonneur detre connue de v
jay cru luy de my adresser avec une parf
confience connoisant combien vous ette
remplis de bonte a obliger nee avec de
qualitee de coeur et des prit digne de
votre naissance pourvay vous me refus
le plaissir de donner ce memoire a son
hattesse royalle je me flatte madame que
ne refuserez pas cette grace a une delle
nee qu un malheur dont sandoute lhitoire
jamais entandu parler reduitte dans une
maison de force pour avoir comte Md
de bethunne de present md de mon malhe
tandresse a toute et pourquoy vous verez par
memoire cy joint cy jay raison de me recri
son injustice mes dame les duchesse de
... et duzce de meusse ont bonne con
omme bien dautre et par son aveu
meme quelle tient de may le tot

Figure 4.7 Page one of letter from Gravelle to the Duchess of Lorge. Photograph by the author.

Source: AB, MS 11769, 419.

> Mlle de Béthune to M. de Monmartel derived from a tenderness that you will see from the *mémoire* that is adjoined to this letter. If I am correct to not receive His justice and that of the Duchesses and Duc [de Monmartel] [which would have been a favor to His direct ancestor] makes me think that it was she that put me in this burning state…[22]

This plea continued for several pages, and in the last part Gravelle pleaded that Lorge ask the king to "take back" his *lettre de cachet*: "Your recommendation would fulfil my wishes would that you could speak with king, more as a father of the people to rescind the *lettre de cachet*."[23] Gravelle's audacity in this letter—demonstrated by writing to a high member of court and referring to the king's authority as that of "a father" before even underscoring his royal authority as the supreme power—was a daring strategy indeed. Appealing to a noble (especially a woman) with a relationship to the king to speak to him on her behalf showed either strength of spirit or a nothing-to-lose attitude.

As the legal brief and collection of documents in the file show, Gravelle continued to write to well-connected members of the court, including daring to address the Comtesse de la Roüle at the queen's palace at Versailles (Figure 4.8). The relationships she cultivated, from the dauphin's valet, to the Comtesse de la Roüle demonstrate that Gravelle tried to communicate with everybody she could ultimately get to the king.

In the next letter presented here (Figure 4.9), we find Gravelle addressing the king himself. Gravelle was accorded the courtesy of being placed in a convent after her first transgression of asking the king/Monmartels for compensation, but she was then transferred to the workhouse for her transgressions of writing and agitating. This is an extraordinary letter, and her directness to the king landed her in prison: first the Bastille and later Vincennes, where she died. It demonstrated a greater degree of audacity and, likely, her frustration that other avenues for seeking justice had not met with success. Her language and tone both decried the injustices perpetrated against her by Béthune and Monmartel.

> *Sire (Votre Majesté)*
> *C'est au throne de la justice et de l'équité que l'innocence opprimée trouve un habile ou abuse de votre autorité et de*

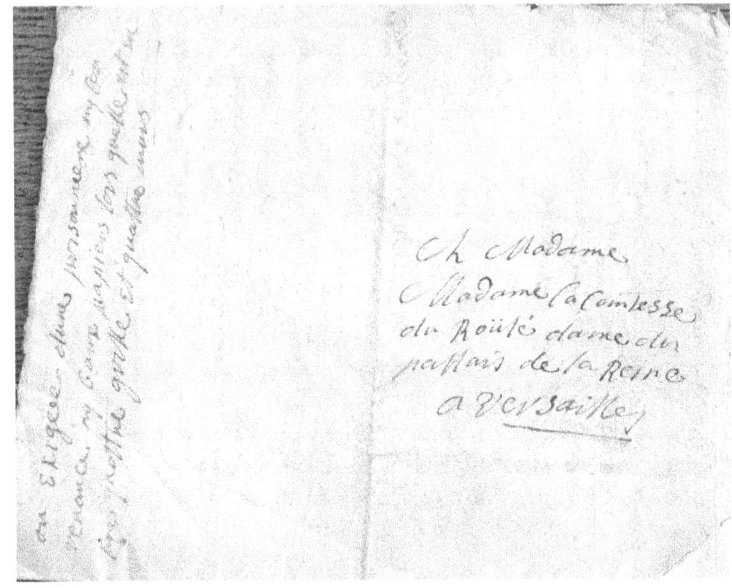

Figure 4.8 Envelope from Gravelle to the Comtesse de la Roüle. Photograph by the author.

Source: AB, MS 11769, folio number missing.

votre confiance pour faire les plus noirs injustices vous et duc Paris de Monmartel et Marquise de Béthune m'en donnent une grave preuve aider par M. Berrier [Berryer] lieutenant de police de Paris.

Cert aux pieds de votre majesté qu'une misérable dans les fers ose s'adresser l'on mertoit depuis près de trois ans dans les maisons de force sans savoir le crime dont je suis occupée.

Sir, (Your Majesty)
It is at the throne of justice and of equity that oppressed innocence has found an easy target where the abuse of your authority and your confidence has committed the most heinous injustices, you and the duc Pâris de Monmartel, (and his wife) Marquise de Béthune give me damning proof aided by M. Berrier, [Berryer] lieutenant of Police of Paris.

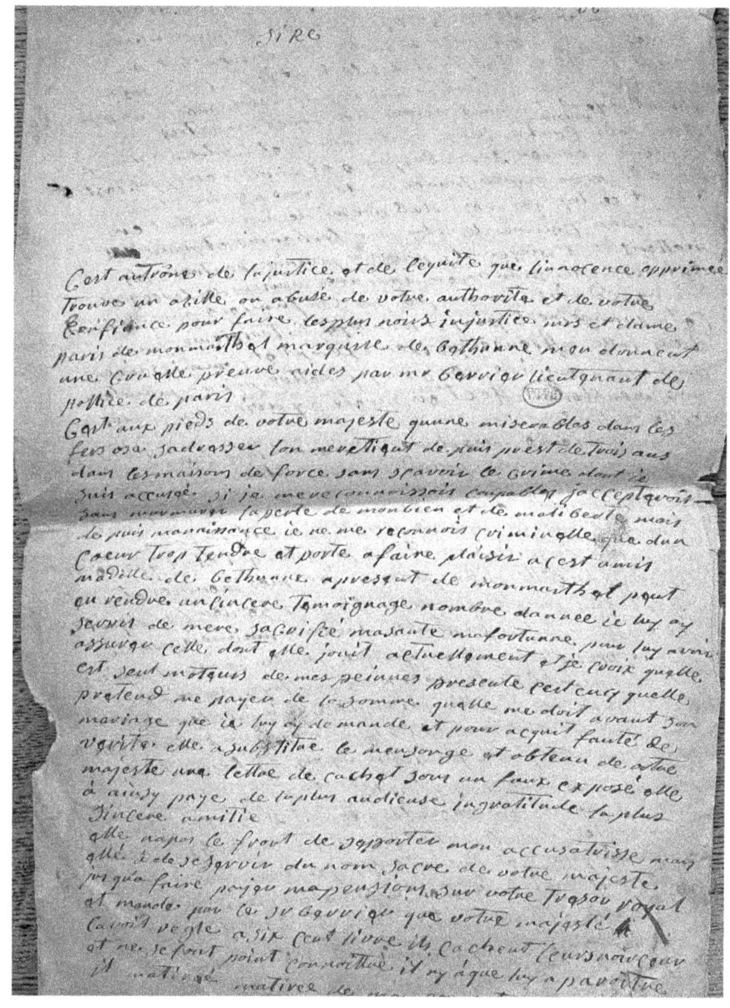

Figure 4.9 Letter from Gravelle to the king. Photograph by the author.

Source: AB, MS 11769, 419.

> Certainly, it is only at the feet of his Majesty that a miserable subject in chains dares to address what has needed to be addressed...after three years in workhouses without knowing the crime for which I am punished.[24]

Gravelle's writing in this letter potentially exposed the corruption infecting the government. She had been admonished and she had received what she perceived as overcorrections, and the reflection of a king that was unnecessarily punitive. She seems to have had confidence in the power of her words and did not appear concerned about their effect on her courtly readership.

The following document is a somber command to transfer Gravelle. It is not only an admonishment but further punishment for her *Mauvaise Conduite*, or bad behavior.

The command to transfer Gravelle signals her threat to the king and a wish to control her unfiltered voice (Figure 4.10). It also exposes the deep embarrassment that the Monmartels continued to express to the king. Nonetheless, Gravelle continued in her pursuit to be heard, no matter how messy or risky. Her wellbeing and already chaotic writing suffered, but she was determined to get her message out.

> *Lundy dernier quinze courans l'officier charge des ordres du Roy pour le transfert de la demoiselle Gravelle à cinq heures du matin, comme il avait ordre de la conduire doucement je luy cessa à apporter toutes les copies de ses mémoires qui sont remplis d'invectives tous sur Madame et Monsieur de Monmartel que vous êtes sur notre communauté ses y ne marque à tous la passion et je ne voie pas qu'il puisse faire aucune sans saisir sur l'esprit des personnes raisonnables.*
>
> *De Montélier, Supérieure de Monastère de la Madelaine. 20 décembre 1749.*
>
> Last Monday the fifteenth, the official in charge of the orders of the king sent by courier for the transfer of Mademoiselle Gravelle at 5am in the morning, as they had the order to gently conduct her and to prohibit her from brining all of the copies of her *mémoires* which were filled with all of the invectives about Madame and Monsieur de Monmartel, that you are ensured our community ignores this emotive

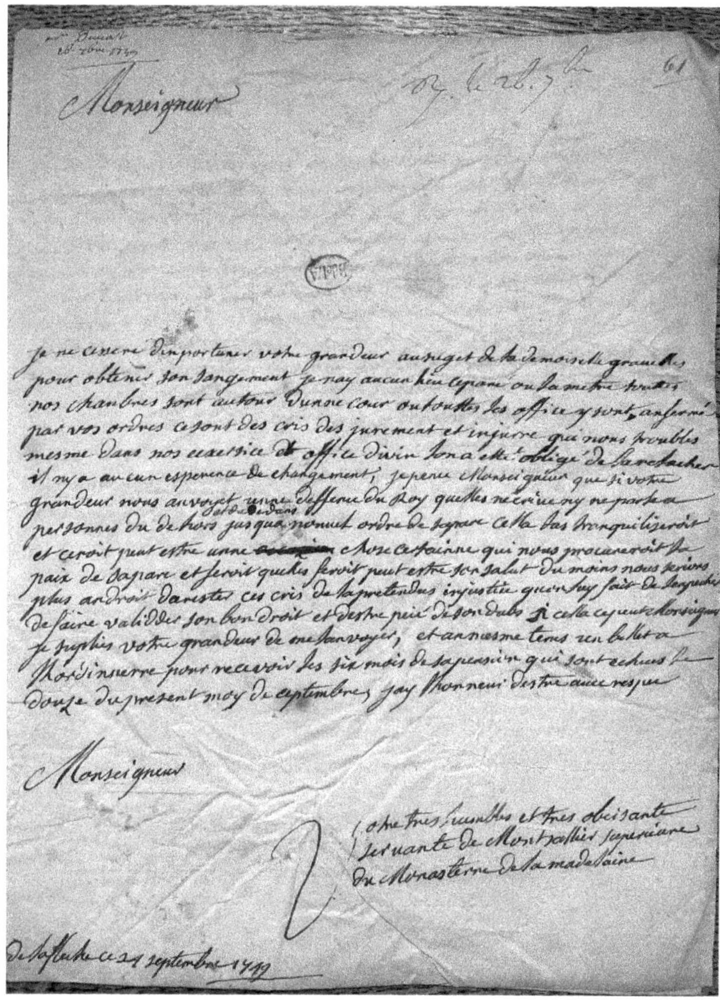

Monseigneur

je ne cessere dinportuner votre grandeur au suiget de la demoiselle gravelle pour obtenir son sangement je nay aucun lieu separe ou la metre toutes nos chambres sont autour dunne cour ou toutes les office y sont, anfermé par vos ordres ce sont des cris des jurement et injurre qui nous troubles mesme dans nos exercice et office divin lon a eté obligé de [illegible] il ny a aucun esperence de changement, jespere Monseigneur que si votre grandeur nous anvoyet unne [illegible] du Roy quelles ne crive ny ne parle a personnes du dehors jusqua nouvel ordre de separe cella las tranquiliseroit et seroit peut estre unne chose certainne qui nous procureroit la paix de la separe et feroit quelle feroit peut estre son salut du moins nous serions plus androit darester ces cris de la pretendus injustice quon luy fait de lempecher de faire valider son bon droit et destre paié de son dubs si cella ce peut Monseigneur je supplie votre grandeur de me lanvoyer, et au mesme tems un billet a lordinairre pour recevoir les six mois de sa pension qui sont echus le douze du present moy de septembre, jay lhonneur destre avec respec

Monseigneur

Votre tres humble et tres obeisante servante de Montpallier superieure du Monastere de la madelaine

De la Fleche ce 21 septembre 17[illegible]

Figure 4.10 Letter from the Mother Superior, most likely a report to the police chief and the king. Photograph by the author.

Source: AB, MS 11769, 419.

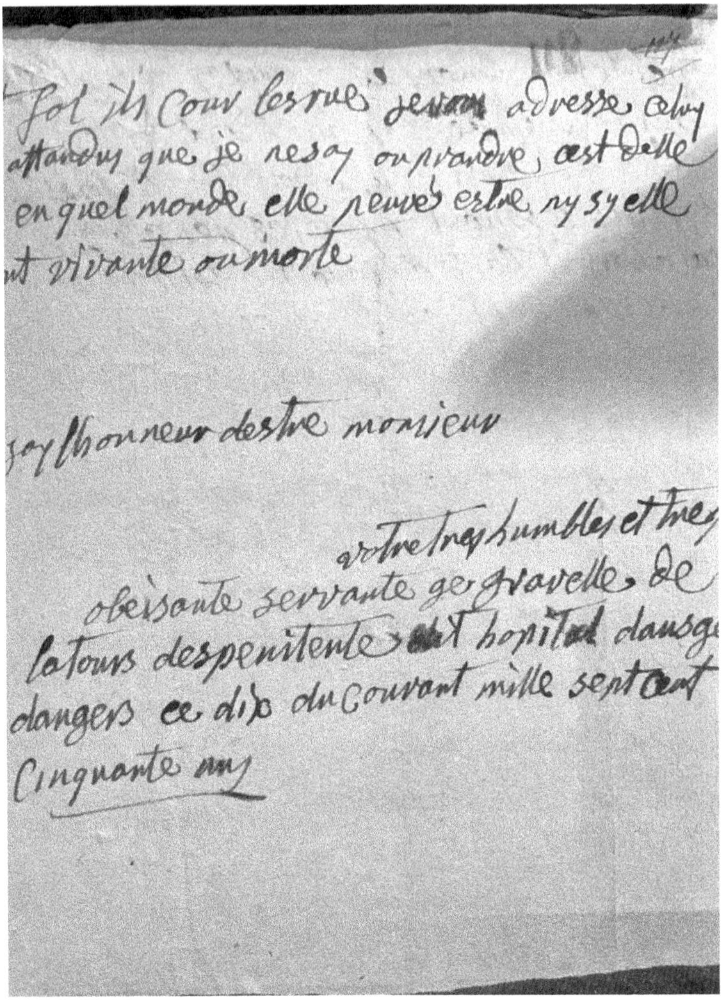

Sol ils Cour les rue jevais adresse celuy
attendu que je ne say ou prandre cest delle
en quel monde elle peuve estre ny sy elle
est vivante ou morte

jay lhonneur destre monsieur

votre tres humble et tres
obeisante servante ge gravelle de
latours des penitente [illegible] hopital dansg
dangers ce dix du Courant mille sept cent
Cinquante ans

Figure 4.11 Letter from Gravelle to the Monmartels. Photograph by the author.

Source: AB, MS 11769, 419.

passion, and I don't see how we can do otherwise than to ask for help from reasonable persons.

The Mother Superior of the monastery of the Madelaine. 20 December 1749.[25]

At the end of a letter from 1750 to the Monmartels (Figure 4.11), Gravelle confessed in the postscriptum,

> *Peut-estre vous aurez peinne a lire ses autres detaille(s) comme je suis sans avoir trop de loisir de finir les mots ny de les penser au racourcir il faut en pareil postitons et ecrire amplement.*
>
> *Pensez-y Monsieur avez-vous peine à lire sans au clair détaille comme je suis sans avoir trop de laisser définir ces mots ny de les penser aux raccourcis il fait en pareil positions et écrire amplement.*
>
> Perhaps you'll have trouble reading these [text indecipherable] details…as I've hardly the leisure to finish or think my words; in such a situation, one must write voluminously.
>
> Think of it, Monsieur, are you having trouble reading without clarity, I have a loss of being able to find the words to define my thoughts, I cannot express them, nor shorten them, so I am in a position just to express them![26]

Here Gravelle admitted that she could not discontinue her thoughts! Her anger and feelings of being a victim of injustice had to be communicated no matter the cost. This kind of unfiltered communication was indeed unusual, and her attempt to communicate at all costs would continue until her death. She would not give up.

The *mémoire* (or grouping of thoughts literally cordoned off with a blue ribbon) presented in her next strategy to communicate was to Monsieur Binet (Figures 4.12–4.15), the first valet of the dauphin and one of the people that Gravelle sought to make part of her networking efforts. She sought to communicate with people of all ranks, so that she may get a message to the king. It demonstrates not only Gravelle's variations in writing and address, but also highlights the diversity of materials present in her file. It was kept as one document, tied together by the blue ribbon seen in the photo.

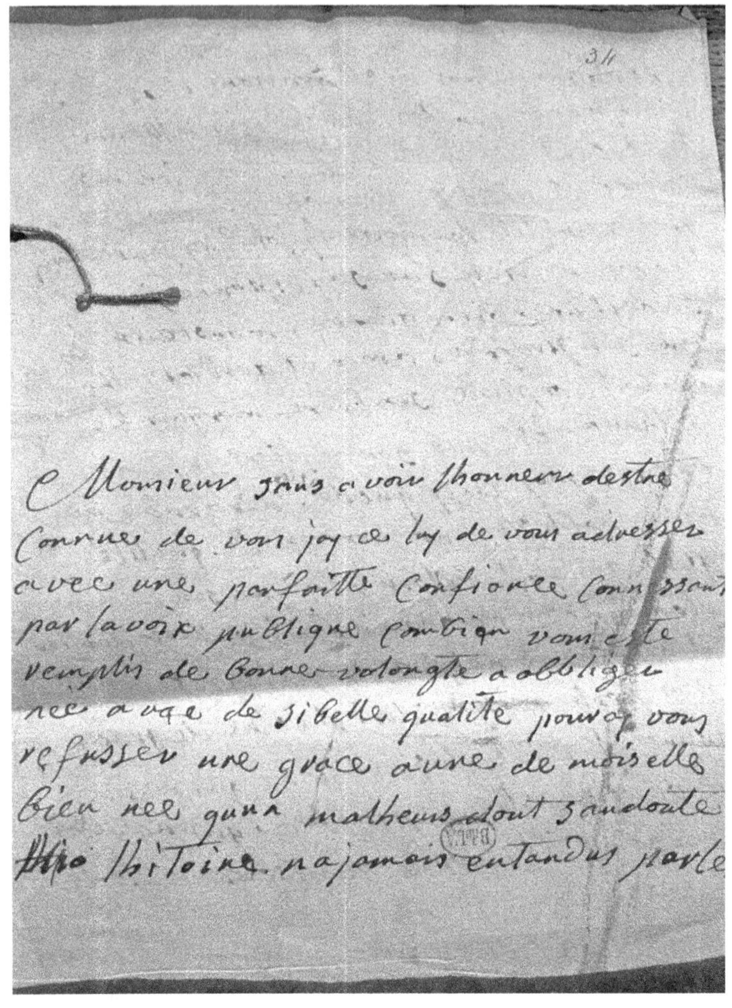

Monsieur sans avoir lhonneur destre
Connue de vous jay ce luy de vous adresser
avec une parfaitte Confiance Connoissant
par la voix publique combien vous este
remplis de bonne volongte a obliger
nee avec de si belle qualite pouvez vous
refusser une grace a une de moiselle
bien nee quun malheurs dont sandoute
lhistoire na jamais entandus parle

Figure 4.12 Page one of letter from Gravelle to Binet, Photograph by the author.

Source: AB, MS 11769, 34.

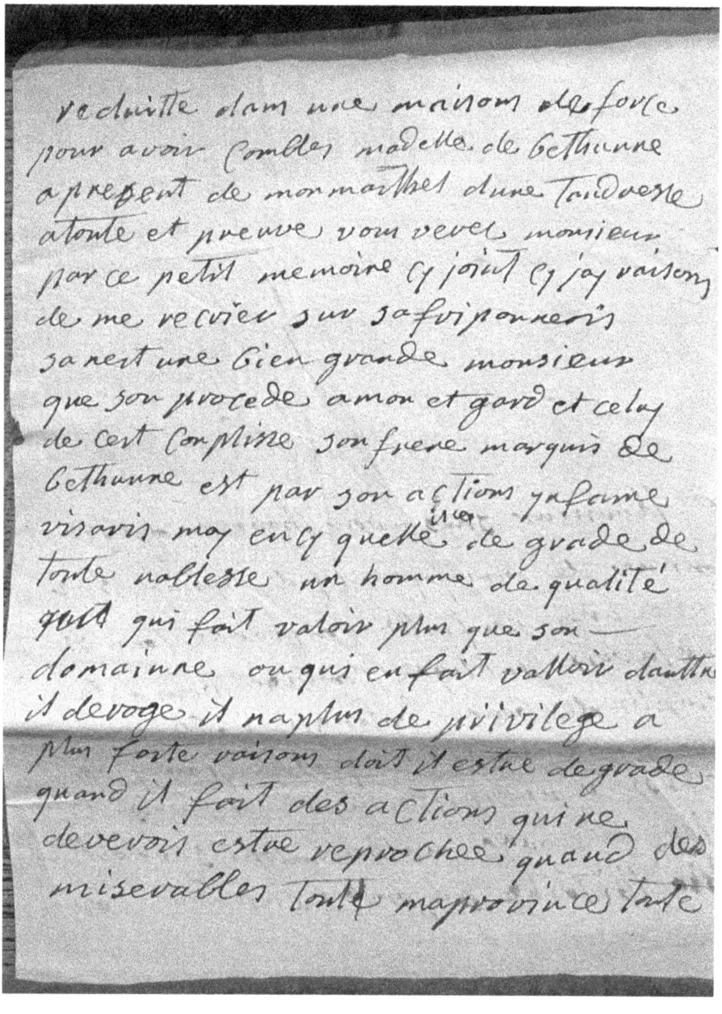

reduitte dans une maison de force
pour avoir comblé madelle de bethunne
a present de mon marthel dune Tendresse
atoute et preuve vous verrez monsieur
par ce petit memoire cy joint cy jay raison
de me recrier sur sa foripounerie
sa nest une bien grande monsieur
que son procede a mon et gard et celuy
de cest complisse son frere marquis de
bethunne est par son actions infame
visavis moy en cy quelle inca de grade de
toute noblesse un homme de qualité
quoy qui fait valoir plus que son —
domainne ou qui en fait valloir dauttre
il deroge il na plus de privilege a
plus forte raison doit il estre degrade
quand il fait des actions qui ne
deveroit estre reprochee quand des
miserables toute ma province tute

Figure 4.13 Page two of letter from Gravelle to Binet. Photograph by the author.

Source: AB, MS 11769, 34.

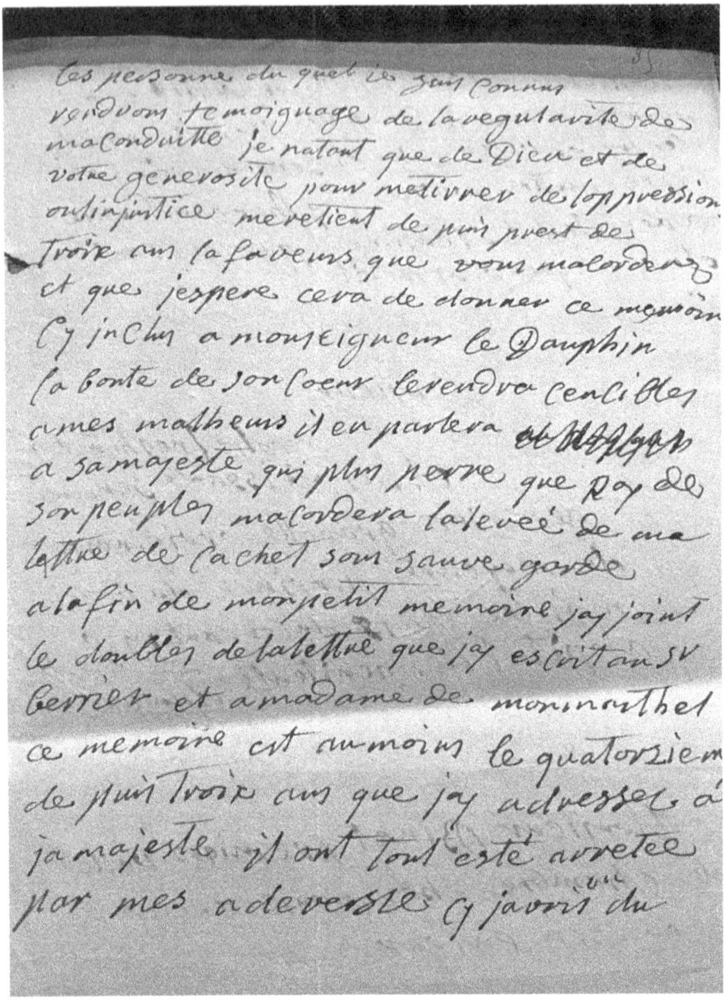

les personne du quel je suis connus
rendrons temoignage de la regularite de
ma conduitte je n'atent que de Dieu et de
votre generosite pour me tirrer de loppression
ou linjustice me retient de puis prest de
Troix ans la faveurs que vous maccorderez
et que jespere cera de donner ce memoire
Cy inclus a monseigneur le Dauphin
la bonte de son coeur le rendra cencibles
a mes malheurs il en parlera ~~[illegible]~~
a sa majeste qui plus perre que Roy de
son peuples maccordera la levee de ma
lettre de cachet sous sauve garde
a la fin de mon petit memoire jay joint
le doubles de la lettre que jay escrit au sr
berrier et a madame de monmarthel
ce memoire est au moins le quatorsiem
de puis troix ans que jay adressee a
sa majeste il ont tout este arretee
par mes adverste cy javois du

Figure 4.14 Page three of letter from Gravelle to Binet. Photograph by the author.

Source: AB, MS 11769, 34.

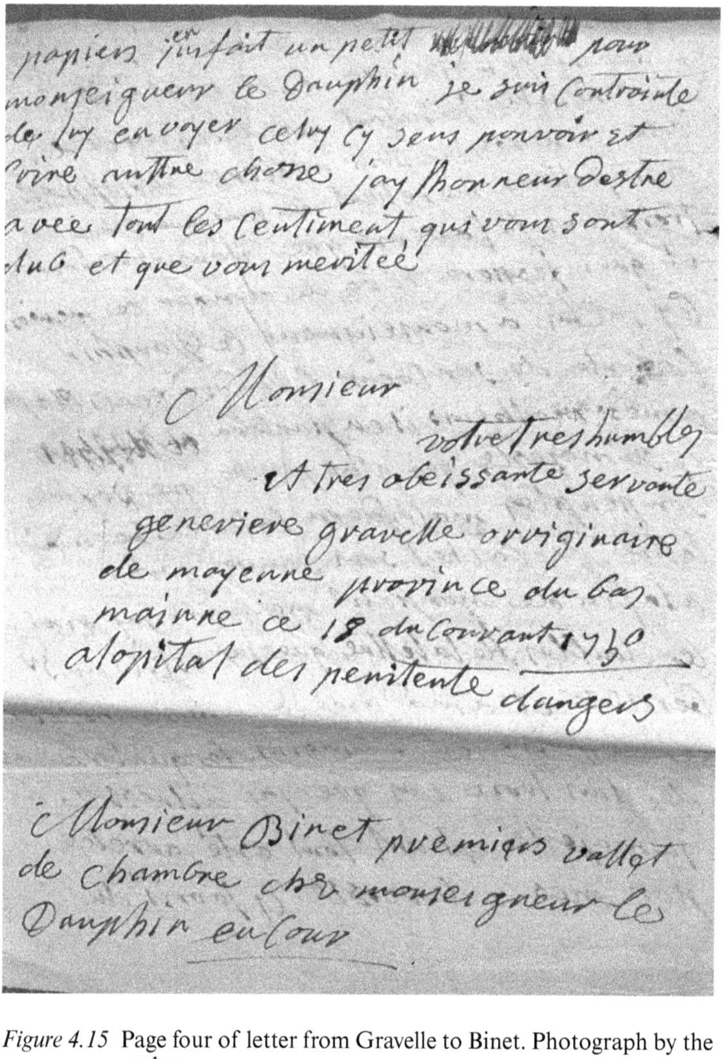

Figure 4.15 Page four of letter from Gravelle to Binet. Photograph by the author.

Source: AB, MS 11769, 34.

A Monsieur Binet, premier valet de chambre chez Monseigneur le dauphin en cour.

Monsieur sans avoir l'honneur d'être connu de vous ; jay ce de jui de vous adresser avec une parfaite confiance connaissant par la voix publique combien vous êtes remplis de bonne volonté à obliger née avec de si belles qualités pour vous refuser une grâce à une demoiselle bien née qu'un malheur dont sans doute l'histoire na jamais entendu parler réduite dans une maison de force pour avoir combler Mademoiselle Béthune à présent de Monmartel d'une tendresse a toute preuve.

Vous avez monsieur par ce petit mémoire ci-joint et j'ai raison de me revoir sure sur friponnerie ca n'est un bien grand monsieur que son procède à mon égard et celui de c'est complice son frère marquis de Béthune est par ses actions infame vis-à-vis moi ainsi quelle c'est dégradé toute noblesse un homme de qualité qui fait valoir plus que son domaine ou qui en fait valait d'entendre qu'il déroge il n'a plus de privilège a plus forte raisons doit être dégradé quand il fait ses actions qui ne devait être reproche quand des misérables toute ma province, toutes les personnes du quel il sont connus rendant témoigne de la régularité de ma conduite, se notant que Dieu et de votre générosité pour me tirer de l'oppression ou l'injustice me retient depuis près de trois ans la faveur que vous m'a accordé et que j'espère sera de donner ce mémoire sy inclus à monsieur le Dauphin.

La bonté de son cœur le rendra sensible âme malheurs il en parlera a sa majesté qui plus père que roy de son peuple m'accordera la levée de ma lettre de cachet sou sauve garde à la fin de mon petit mémoire j'ai joint le doublet de la lettre que j'ai écrit en M. Beyyrier et a Mme de Marmonthel ce mémoire est au moins the quatorzième depuis trois ans que j'adresse à sa majesté et ils ont tous été arrêtée par mes adressée ici joint papiers en fait un petit pour monsieur le dauphin je suis contrainte de luy envoyer celui sy sans pouvoir croire mettre chose j'ai l'honneur d'être à tous les sentiments qui vous sont dus et que vous méritée (méritez).

Monsieur

Votre très humble et très obéissante servante

Geneviève de Gravelle originaire de Mayenne province du bas Mayenne ce 18 couvant 1750.

A l'hôpital des pénitentes d'Angers

Without having the honor of having met, I do have the honor of addressing you in perfect confidence, knowing by public opinion how well you are respected for being endowed with good will and you would necessarily be of such refined nature that you would not refuse a demoiselle of high status the grace and treatment she is due, and certainly you have been apprised of the misfortune she has suffered and now finds herself in reduced circumstances and is placed in a workhouse, all for having shown Mlle de Béthune and M. de Monmartel kindness at every turn.

You have here monsieur by way of this little *mémoire* attached to this file, and I have reason to believe that it is by a great miscalculation that it is not a noble man that moves forward on my behalf, but it is the complicit brother, the Marquis de Béthune and by his horrible actions against me it is possible to see how the nobility of a man of quality, can be worth more than his domain…please give this *mémoire* to the Dauphin.

The goodness of his heart makes his soul sensitive to the misfortunes, and he will speak on this more as a father than as a king to his people and to please agree to remove the letter de cachet attached and saved to the last part of my little *mémoire* that I joined the copy of my letter that I wrote to M. Beryyier [Berryer] to Mme Monmartel (née Béthune) is at least the fourteenth one since three years I address his Majesty and all my missives have been halted, including the attached papers, one little one that was addressed to the dauphin, I am upset to have sent him this without believing this would pose a problem. It is my honor to offer you all the sentiments that are owed to you and that you merit.

Sir,

Your very humble and very obedient servant,

Genevieve de Gravelle, from Mayenne, province of lower Mayenne from the Convent of the Penitents of Angers, 18…1750.[27]

Some of her words were poorly chosen and at times incomprehensible, yet her accusation, the vocabulary of her feelings of betrayal, and the rupture in her noble sensibility and code of ethics were expressed rather poignantly.

Gravelle continued to write to Béthune in 1751, as evidenced by Figure 4.16. Gravelle appears to have been pushed further into her

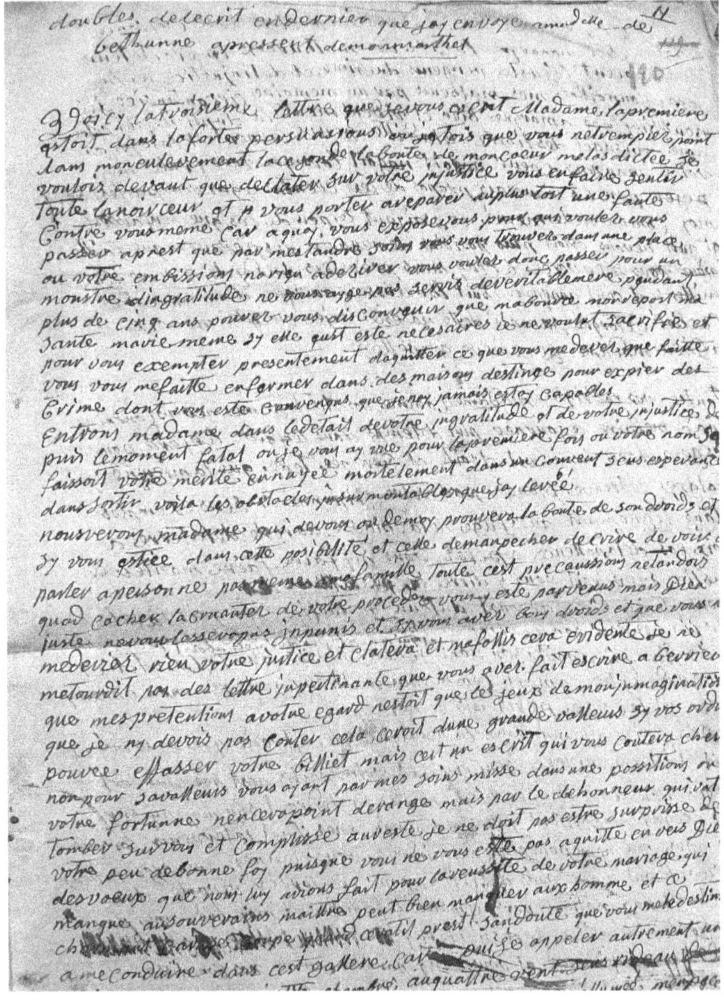

doubles de lecrit en dernier que jay envoye a madelle de
bethunne apresent a demonmarthe

Figure 4.16 Letter from Gravelle to Mme de Béthune. Photograph by the author.

Source: AB, MS 11769, 120.

own decline. She could not accept the rejection, nor could she tolerate being ignored—perhaps she could not tolerate being invisible and unheard. This letter attests that she was begging for attention. Sometimes the responses to her network connections and members of the court were personalized. The missives to Béthune and the Marquise de Pompadour to pay attention to her were not response letters, but pleas to release her from her confinement. Below are some further reflections from Gravelle's confinement when she is sent to the Angers workhouse.

> *Le voici la troisième lettre que je vous écris Madame. La première éstoit dans la forte persuasion ou j'éstois que vous ne trempier point dans mon enlèvement la (se) fonde de la bonté de mon cœur me las dictée je voulais devant que d'éclater sur votre injustice vous enfaite sentir toute la(le) noirceur et portez à réparer de plus tost (a plus tôt) une faute contre vous-même car à quoy vous exposer vous trouver dans une place ou votre embissions (ambitions) ne risque rien à dériver vous voulez donc passer pour un monstre d'ingratitude.*
>
> *Entrons madame dans ce détail de votre ingratitude et de votre injustice depuis le moment fatal ou je vous ay vue pour la première fois ou votre nom ce qui faisait votre mérite ennuyé mortellement dans un couvent sans espérance d'en sortir voilà les obstacles insurmontables que j'ay levée.* [28]
>
> And it is the third time that I write to you Madame. The first time was under the great impression that you were not aware of (nor involved in) my being taken away. From the bottom of my heart, I had wanted to communicate with you, and for you to be aware of the darkness of your injustice so that you could repair it as soon as possible, so as not to expose you nor must you be exposed or put you in a vulnerable position for your ambitions. I know that you do not want to risk anything, nor to be perceived of as an ungrateful monster.[29]
>
> Let us enter, Madame, into the details of your ingratitude, of your injustice, from the fateful moment that I saw you the first time, when your name alone gave you merit, bored to death in a convent without any hope of leaving it, here are the insurmountable obstacles that I have helped you to overcome.[30]

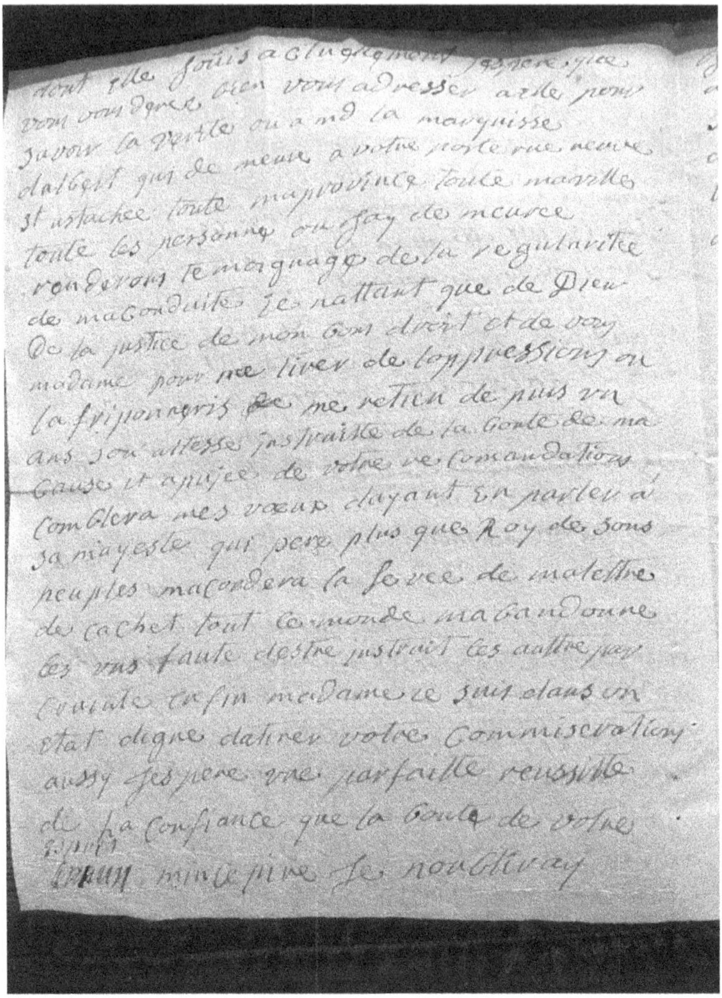

Figure 4.17 Last letter from Gravelle to Béthune. Photograph by the author.

Source: AB, MS 11769, 120.

This missive was repetitive and purposeful, the urgency of Gravelle's situation producing what has been referred to by Wingrove as "an excess" of emotions.[31] At first, Gravelle credited Béthune with the possibility of having been unaware of her incarceration: "The first time was under the great impression that you were not aware of (nor involved in) my being taken away."[32] But then she named the "ingratitude" of Béthune directly. Her tone was angry and lacked the contrition of her previous letters, as she directly accused Béthune of being an opportunist and taking advantage of Gravelle's goodwill and connections: "…of your injustice, from the fateful moment that I saw you the first time."[33] Sometimes her letters revealed a strategic or self-reflexive awareness of their own rhetorical tactics, and sometimes they expressed personal outrage that may have proven to be self-destructive.

Gravelle then expressed her outrage in a manner that was unquestioningly meant to strike Béthune directly: "[W]hen your name alone gave you merit, bored to death in a convent without any hope of leaving it, here are the insurmountable obstacles that I have helped you to overcome."[34] Gravelle was without a doubt invoking the point that she was of a higher class and status than Béthune, whom she helped climb the social ladder. The social ladder had implicit noble values and manners. To Gravelle, Béthune's behavior was unbecoming, and there were social expectations to which Béthune did not adhere. Béthune's acts were ignoble and therefore monstrous.

We can see how Gravelle's resistance took shape in the substantial number of letters she managed to produce from the workhouse and convent of Angers. She concludes, "I also feel I don't know anything anymore" (Figure 4.17).[35]

Though Gravelle's intention may not have been to leave a story for posterity, the trove of letters and forensic storytelling that she left behind gives us access to her voice, as well as those of a great many other women from her time. The work of piecing together and interpreting the noise and the mess is an attempt to construct, tell, and retell a narrative. The medium of the letter itself presents us with a distinctive set of literary tropes. Is the material presence of the letter metonymic or synecdoche in that it represents a part of a holistic account of the state of women confined against their will? The messiness and chaos reflect a society in which women were not able to communicate with the public in a meaningful way, save for scandals representative of the system's dysfunction.[36] The above letters were an enactment of authorial power through which Gravelle asserted herself. The act of writing insinuated a dialog with the king and others who were not her social or political equals.[37]

The entirety of Gravelle's file offers insight into how her writing was not only an act of anger but also one of resistance. In addition, we are invited to "read" the objects in her file and understand them as both a literary product and a political tool. The act of writing was necessary for Gravelle's physical and mental survival. This is significant as there were complaints about the volume of her writing from early on. Yes, Gravelle's grammar was bad, her spelling not great, but her sense of purpose was clear—these letters may have been poorly written, but they were in fact well aimed. Regarding the question of legibility, Wingrove asks, "How do we read the letters if we are to read them at all?"[38] Feminist scholarship must expand this question by asking, "How do we read the *entire file*?" Gravelle's often repetitive and rambling writing poses obstacles to legibility, but nevertheless it is rich in forensic and material contextuality. The most fruitful approach to understanding Gravelle's case is to deepen our understanding of her file's forensics by examining the material objects therein, an approach that raises the issue of quantity yet perhaps not quality.

When looking at the negative commentaries made on the style of women's letter writing in previous scholarship and of these letters, we ought to consider Gravelle's possible goals. There is an interesting fluctuation between the formality Gravelle wished to convey as part of her loyalty to and belonging within the nobility and her desperate self-expression, the latter of which was not self-conscious and was at times even vulgar (such as in her repetition and the multiple copies she made with only slight variations).[39] Yet, the demonstration of her unraveling through the chaos of her writing and the volume of letters in her file have the capacity to move new readers of her story.

Here we are reading literature that reflected resistance and protest and told the story of a life in confinement. The sad post-scriptural placement of Gravelle's description and qualification demonstrates the paradox of improvising with a form of expression wherein authority rested on conventionality.[40] We observe the escalation of her frustration as she advanced in age and her living conditions worsened. The letters ended after 359 pages with a reference to the 43 years Gravelle had spent in confinement—in convents, workhouses, and prisons. Gravelle's confinement in the Château de Vincennes seems to have brought an end to her epistolary output. Along with all the other components of her file, the reader can see and understand the message: Gravelle's experience was that of a lifestyle imposed on a woman with little to no power. Her file documents reflected her attempts to gain empowerment and agency by writing and reacting to her forced confinement, a fact that should not be lost or ignored, just as her behavior should not be relegated to "being crazy." There is nothing insane about writing prolifically, especially if it is one's only means of obtaining agency.

Notes

1 "Letters and memoirs addressed to the king, members of the nobility, and presidents of various *parlements* continued to surface over the next two years; a third *lettre de cachet* was requested and issued, this time ordering her transfer to the Bastille. Gravelle's confinement in the château reserved for political prisoners seem to have brought an end to her epistolary output; records indicate that a fourth *lettre de cachet* ordering her transfer to Vincennes two years later was prompted by overcrowding at the Bastille." Elizabeth Wingrove, "Sovereign Address," *Political Theory* 40, no. 2 (2012): 136.

2 "Almost immediately after being detained, Gravelle began writing letters decrying the injustice of her situation. Passed by hand and deposited at the post by sympathetic or bribed residents of the monastery, her narratives of aristocratic abuse and the disregard for her "good right" began circulating in Paris." Ibid.

3 "The monastery officials in charge of Gravelle's care requested and received an order prohibiting her from all writing. But the missives continued to appear." Ibid.

4 When considering this form of justice meted out by the king by the *lettres de cachet*, Arlette Farge and Michel Foucault have shown that noble and bourgeois families made extensive use of them as a supplement to parental power right up to the Revolution; by midcentury, they had become a potent symbol of absolutism's excesses. See *Le Désordre des familles: Lettres de cachet des Archives de la Bastille au XVIIIe siècle* (Paris: Gallimard, 2014). Unlike the *lettre patente* (which was

typically addressed to a *parlement,* always sent uncacheted, and, once registered, was published for general dissemination as the law of the land), the secrecy of the *lettre de cachet* underwrote concerns about its political propriety: who knew what the letter's contents might be? Who knew whether the information initiating it was accurate? Who even knew whether the king himself had signed it?

5 Paris, Archives de la Bastille (AB), MS 11769, 18.

6 "And in the end, such excess will always elude interpretive order. The agonizingly indecipherable writing, the unknown number of uncaptured letters that circulated 'freely,' her failure to submit to the grammatical partitions of language: Gravelle's cries must to some extent remain 'blind and blinding,' But this lack of mastery does not leave her dumb, nor does our incomplete reception leave us deaf. Indeed, the felicity in Gravelle's unhappy performatives lies not in how they reveal historical impediments to political speech, but in how they bespeak a politics that is simultaneously material and literary, expressive and strategic, excessive and never quite enough '…just as I have said in the memoir included here, not being able to explain myself *vive voix*.'" Wingrove, "Sovereign Address," 156-157.

7 Joseph Omer Joly de Fleury (1715-1810) is notable for his strong opposition to the *philosophes* and the publication of the *Encyclopédie* in 1759. Originally from Burgundy and a noble himself, he was from the distinguished Joly de Fleury family. A significant number of members of this family were leading French magistrates and officials under the *Ancien Régime*. His political acumen was unparalleled, and his reactionary stance seems even more relevant today because of his ban on inoculation against smallpox in June 1763.

8 "Sovereign Address," 136. Police Chief Berryer's name was spelled in many different variations throughout the documents. Depending on the author of the document, it may have been sounded out or transcribed. It is found in many the files under the following variants: Berrier. Berryier, Beryyier.

9 Nancy Miller, *The Poetics of Gender* (New York: Columbia University Press, 1986).

10 For a full explanation of the phenomenon, see Dena Goodman, *Becoming a Women in the Age of Letters* (Ithaca: Cornell University Press, 2009), 41.

11 "But even as she attempts the difficult task of attacking the *lettre de cachet* without directly undermining the sovereignty it enacts, Gravelle persistently pushes the latter to its limits. Biblical allusion makes the case indirectly. Likening Mme de Monmartel to Jezebel and herself to Naboth, she evokes the story of an innocent landowner lured to his death by false letters from the king, Ahab, who received a dooming

judgment from the prophet Elijah as a consequence. It was of course all Jezebel's doing (she wrote the letters and sent them out under the king's seal) but ignorance on Ahab's part didn't save him." Wingrove, "Sovereign Address," 152-153.

12 As Goodman attests, there is a naturalness to women's letter writing. *Becoming a Woman*, 140.

13 Wingrove, "Sovereign Address," 136.

14 Ibid., 137.

15 Ibid. See also 159, footnote 15, where Wingrove states, "Seizing one's personal papers along with one's person was standard practice in the case of criminal and political detentions. Impounded writings were bundled and closed with the detainee's cachet, or more commonly, when they didn't have one, sealed with a paper that included both his or her signature and the detaining officer's; the papers were returned to the prisoner upon their release. While this procedure was followed when Gravelle was taken into custody, there is every indication that she recorded copies of her illicit letters on older letters from the sealed bundle."

16 "And the sensory challenges faced by properly *literary* analysts are multiple. The 'blind and blinding speech' that confounds historiographers, for example, suggests words that lack and impair vision. Certainly, the phrase captures an aspect of the experience of reading Gravelle: the hundreds of pages of her letters weave in and out of legibility and grammaticality, while their materiality—smudged ink, torn pages, new prose written besides, around, and over old prose on the letters she sometimes used as stationary—strains and occasionally bewilders the reader." Ibid., 138.

17 See Chapter 1 for an explanation of the convent versus the workhouse.

18 Wingrove, "Sovereign Address," 141.

19 Ibid.

20 "Women write oceans of letters, but most of the ones published are only of limited value in helping us to understand letter writing as it was practiced by 'ordinary' women in their daily lives, or how it might have functioned in the articulation of their gendered subjectivity." Goodman, *Becoming a Woman*, 5.

21 "Both Gravelle's historical situation and my desire to retrieve it illustrate the interdependence of Rancière's methodological, political, and aesthetic critiques: to read and so re-count her hinges on a re-partitioning of audible and visual orders, in her own time and perhaps in ours." Wingrove, "Sovereign Address," 138.

22 Ibid.

23 The letter also includes these accusatory concluding lines: "*Tout le monde m'abandonne les vus faute d'être instruit les autres par cruauté*

enfin madame je suis dans un état digne d'attirer votre commiseration…" Translation: "Everybody has abandoned me, and they are cruelly instructed by others finally Madame I am in a state that merits your commiseration…" All translation and transcription by the author unless otherwise stated. Ibid.

24 Ibid., 36.
25 Ibid., 61.
26 Ibid., 118.
27 Ibid.
28 Ibid.
29 Ibid. Translation mine.
30 Ibid. Translation by Wingrove, "Sovereign Address," 147.
31 Wingrove, "Sovereign Address," 156.
32 AB, MS 11769, 120. "*La première éstoit dans la forte persuasion ou j'éstois que vous ne trempier point dans mon enlèvement.*"
33 Ibid. "*De votre injustice depuis le moment fatal ou je vous ay vue pour la première fois.*"
34 Ibid. "*[V]otre nom ce qui faisait votre mérite ennuyé mortellement dans un couvent sans espérance d'en sortir voilà les obstacles insurmontables que j'ay levée.*"
35 Ibid., folio number illegible.
36 "Among these provocations is a reconsideration of the place of literary interpretation in the field. On the one hand, close attention to prose content and form, if not the particular practice of something called 'close reading,' is regularly reputed to political theorists as a whole. Likewise our canonical texts are generally recognized as literary creations, even as issues of genre can trouble the general recognition… On the other hand, the field's multiple appropriations of language theory—in the form of discourse ethics and speech act theory more generally—tend to privilege the epistemological and ontological implications of language systems; rarely dwelling long at the sites of an utterance's production, this work typically presupposes the existence of 'voice' that literary analysis renders problematic." Wingrove, "Sovereign Address," 138.
37 Ibid., 141.
38 "This is of course a vexed issue, whether the text and author in question are canonical or obscure." Ibid., 139.
39 However, I also ascribe to the theory that writing cannot necessarily be read through the lens of authorial intention.
40 "Here Gravelle's desire to capitalize on the visual ease and temporal horizon of print isn't signaled as a desire to 'go public': couched in terms of making her prose legible and her account perceptible to addressees, her request signals conformity to the limited circulation of private letters." Wingrove, "Sovereign Address," 142.

References

AB, MS 11769, (Gravelle)

Farge, Arlette and Michel Foucault. *Le Désordre des familles: Lettres de cachet des Archives de la Bastille au XVIIIe siècle*. Paris: Gallimard, 2014.

Goodman, Dena. *Becoming a Women in the Age of Letters*. Ithaca: Cornell University Press, 2009.

Miller, Nancy. *The Poetics of Gender*. New York: Columbia University Press, 1986.

Wingrove, Elizabeth. "Sovereign Address." *Political Theory* 40, no. 2 (2012): 135–164.

5 "What's in a Name?"

The Case of Angélique Schwab

It is well documented that in eighteenth-century France, the institution of the convent provided a convenient means for some families and for society as a whole, to rid themselves of problematic individuals—as in the previously examined case of Geneviève de Gravelle.[1] Alternatively, for some women the convent was a haven and a means of achieving a degree of autonomy and freedom. In this analysis, Glucka Schwab (later known as Angélique Schwab) resisted the patriarchal authority of her father through her conversion to Catholicism. In eighteenth-century France, authority began with the king, who dictated his supreme governance through the patriarch of the family. Patriarchal authority, especially in the Jewish community, was left to rabbinical control and, more directly, to fathers and men in the community. The king approved the rabbis as community leaders, thus leaving matters to his personally selected leaders as a direct means of governance. I endeavor to trace a line from the king's authority to Glucka's father and conclude that she was resisting patriarchal authority by converting to Catholicism. Paradoxically in this case, the king helped her escape her filial obligations. Sadly, Glucka's resistance ultimately proved fatal.

Angélique Schwab's story, though unique in many respects, illustrates the dynamics and mechanisms of patriarchal authority and feminine resistance that we see throughout this book. In this case study, as in those others we have discussed, we weigh the historical documents and evaluate the information therein to gain a better understanding of the ability of women with limited choices to achieve a degree of autonomy. The testimony of her

DOI: 10.4324/9780429001147-6

brother and her memoirs provide context for the backdrop of her story. Letters from the magistrate, the clergy, and the court give more solid evidence of the thesis of this chapter. Certain documents provide some clarity about Angélique's pathway to the convent. The story we are able to recover has been woven together from various documents, principally those drawn from the Archives of the Bastille and from the Archives Israelites from 1729. Although this cache of documents is disorganized and other evidence is hard to find, the discovered ensemble still provides the skeleton of the tale. By consulting the forensic evidence that is available, including the file brief and the other extant historical accounts, we can see the framework of a compelling and significant story.

A Brief History of the Jews in Eighteenth-Century Paris

Our framing of the story of Glucka, ultimately leading to her conversion to Catholicism and her name change to Angélique, is rooted in the history of the Jews of Metz and their migration to Paris. From the beginning of the eighteenth century, Jews in Paris were required to live in specified neighborhoods, still referred to as ghettos.[2] This medieval practice, originally designed to "protect" Jews from the violence of the mob, constituted a significant disability and impeded their inclusion in French society in most respects. What a conundrum and what an impossible position to be a marginalized people at the heart of such a great city! The neighborhoods to which Jews were restricted included the quarters of Paris that are still centers for various activities considered traditional Jewish trades, such as textile and artisanal manufacturing, wholesale trade in spirits, and the import and export of goods. The areas of St Martin, St Denis, Beaubourg, and Haut Marais were parts of the city where Jews lived together in great density. They were concentrated in two ghettos, the Allemands in the St Martin, St Denis neighborhood, and the Espagnols in the St Germain, St André neighborhood. At times, certain Jews of exceptional wealth and status could legally dwell outside the ghetto gates. But the institution of residence restrictions, especially for Jews of Alsatian and Ashkenazic descent, persisted in France until the French Revolution, and punitive taxation continued to be imposed on

Ashkenazic Jews until well after the French Revolution.[3] In some cases, Ashkenazic Jews were relocated from Metz to Paris to live close to the city quarters of the aristocracy, available to serve any moneylending needs. Despite their proximity to the gentile population, Jews were for the most part excluded from any social interaction with the general population of Paris. In the police records of the Archives de la Bastille, most files that involve Jews bear the label "*Juif de Metz*," referring directly to the subject's Ashkenazi origins and roots in the region of Metz.[4]

As early files indicate, it became standard practice to obligate Jews to hold passports to reside in Paris. In the mid-eighteenth century, the civic authorities of Paris charged Monsieur Bautry, a special agent of the king and appointee to the police task force, with the establishment of "*un projet pour ne laisser aucun juif sans passeport*," or "a project to force Jews to hold special self-identifying passports."[5] The function of this special agent's position was left undefined by the king, yet according to the files in the archives, Bautry seems to have held the official role of "Jew-finder." The king's special agents were typically deployed throughout Paris to keep control of the Jews. Bautry suggested policies to the king regarding this disliked yet economically indispensable ethnic group.

Many Jews were identified in criminal records and other official documents of the period simply as *juif*. In fact, *juif*, or Jew, was written as the label of the criminal proceedings, as though being Jewish were somehow a contributing cause of the crime.[6] The reports show that Jews were considered "prolific suspects," responsible for all sorts of transgressions. As Leon Kahn asserts, they were labeled as "*juifs suspects nombreux*."[7] Jews were not only disliked and viewed with suspicion, but they were also legally precluded from practicing most professions.[8]

We can find reports from police chiefs D'Argenson and Hérault dating from 1725 to 1739. Next, Marville became police chief from 1739 to 1747, and then Berryer was named *lieutenant general de police* in 1747. He was reputedly the harshest chief of police regarding the treatment of Jews in Paris during the eighteenth century. It was Berryer who oversaw and enforced the system of internal passports to control and limit Jews' activities. Though the king appointed and approved the rabbis in France and reinforced the father's position as supreme authority in the family, the police chiefs (who carried out the justice of the king) were the true masters of the Jewish population in Paris.

We can locate records of only two Jewish women in the Archives of the Bastille reported as having converted to the Catholic faith. One was Manon Lévy, converted by a priest at St Eustache and placed in a home to learn to make carpets. She did not fare well, eventually being deemed "insane" and confined to a hospital. We know little of her situation or her relationship to her family and community. The second case, which is both more problematic and of greater interest to our study, is that of Glucka-Angélique Schwab.

Schwab's family name is recorded in many spelling variants in the factum. As spelling in French was barely standardized at the time, it is not surprising that transliterations from Yiddish varied greatly. The surname that we know today as Schwab was also spelled *Schouabe* and *Chouabe*.[9] When referring to the historical documents, I transcribe the name as recorded in the file, but when speaking of the Schwab family, I use the modern spelling. I refer to Glucka-Angélique as Glucka until 1729, after which I switch to her adopted name, Angélique. Later, we will see two variants in her record: she would also be known as *Olique*, possibly a diminutive of Angélique.

The king generally assisted in the appointment of the local rabbi, who acted as the authority for the Jewish community. The rabbi was often a political appointment and a liaison between the Jewish community and the crown. One would think Jewish women were generally spared antisemitic interactions with the public, as their existence was not very public-facing and because of the rabbi's role as the patrilocal authority, but this is not the case. In fact, the antisemitism and misogyny of the age led to increased hatred towards Jewish women. As Kahn says, "The women were not spared, all Jews were people to be exiled, they were 'bad subjects' who were best purged from the city of Paris."[10]

As we begin weaving together the story of Angélique from the assembled files, let us consult the family tree that provides us with an idea of the contemporaneous network of some of the Jewish families from Metz. Jews did not marry outside of their religion, and for the most part they did not find marriage partners outside of their own social networks (which may however have extended to other countries within the Ashkenazic world). It is likely that a match for Glucka would have been arranged when she was in her early teens.

Jewish Community Network and Names of the Connected Families

- Family Tree of Glucka "Angélique" Schwab, born c.1711. Deceased c.1732.[11]
  - Parents
    - Ruben "Rouben" "Schwaube" Schwab, born c.1680. Deceased 17 November 1737, aged about 57 years old. Banquier. Married 11 August 1694 to Hintié Brune "Anne" Hindchen Levy, born c.1680. Deceased 3 March 1758, aged about 78 years old.
  - Siblings
    - Abraham Ruben Schwab (c.1707–1741).
    - Elie Ruben Schwab (c.1710–1748). Married 19 July 1739 to Breinlé Levy (c.1717–1748).
    - Agathe Jaket "Schwaube" Schwab (c.1713–1747). Married to Gershon Jacob Cahen (d.1758).
    - Juda Judic Zadoc Ruben "Judique" Zadok Schwab (c.1715–1784). Married 7 February 1732 to Agathe Jakette Schwab (c.1715–1765). Married 19 November 1765 to "Julie" Jutlé Halphen (1748–1823).
    - Beillé Babette Elisabeth Schwab (1717–1772). Married 27 March 1739 to Alcan Abraham Alcan.
    - Abraham Halenbourg Halimbourg (c.1715–1772).
    - Rachel Schwab (1729–1730).
  - Paternal Grandparents, Uncles, and Aunts
    - Abraham Mayer Schwaube Schwab (c.1640–1704). Married Jaket "Jachet" Agathe Yochet Gompertz Clèves (d.1709).
    - Jacob Abraham "Jean-Charles" Schwaube "Schwab" (c.1665/70-1729). He had five children but no mention of the wife/wives.[12]

In addition to the family relationships recorded here, Glucka's family had close ties to the prominent rabbi Joseph of Worms.

According to the historian Arthur Hertzberg, Joseph of Worms was the favored rabbi of Louis XV. It is evident that the king placed patriarchal/patrilocal confidence and authority squarely on Joseph's shoulders.[13] The Schwab family was implicated in an incident described in the documents relating to Jacob of Worms the son of Joseph. Jacob of Worms and Abraham Schwab, the former being a Metz banker and an army purveyor, spent significant time in Paris, though without the proper habitation permits. Jacob of Worms, despite his important commercial role and connections, was arrested for practicing Judaism in a secret synagogue in a Paris apartment, and the two Torah scrolls he had in his possession were confiscated. He was held in the Bastille together with Samuel Lévy, his co-conspirator and a man of influence.[14] These two men managed to pay off the guards and have kosher meat brought to them, and they were also allowed to pray together in prison.

The case file of Abraham Schwab helps to clarify the context of the Schwab family, as well as the Jews of Metz, their existence in Paris, and their relationship to the court and king. We find a separate document in the archives of the prisoners of the Bastille labeled "*Juifs Prison: Oct 1729.*" Abraham was accused by a woman, Marie le Fevre, of swindling her out of 800 livres by not delivering her goods. He was arrested by the police, and a story unfolds of his imprisonment with the other individuals rounded up by the new police chief, or "Jew-finder". Significantly, Jacob of Worms and Samuel Lévy were in the Bastille when Abraham Schwab was imprisoned. As we can see in the archives, Jacob of Worms wrote letters on behalf of Abraham, asking the king to exonerate him.[15] It is also recorded that the king had earlier supported Elie Schwab, the grandfather of Abraham, in becoming rabbi for the Jews of Metz in 1721.[16]

Abraham Schwab

The file that precedes Angélique Schwab's in the archive's catalog (not only alphabetically but chronologically by one month), is that of "*Abraham Schouabe juif.*" It appears that there were familial ties that connected the family to the famous *Affaire Schouabe*, in which Jacob Schwab, probably Abraham's uncle, was accused of *banqueroute* (financial fraud).

The first of these factums begins the storytelling from a materialistic and evidentiary viewpoint. It contains a letter to the lieutenant general of police, Hérault, from Langlade, who was part of the police unit comprised of spies whom Hérault chose and directed to do his bidding.[17]

Marie le Fevre was a linen merchant from Paris who owed money to "*Chouabe juif*" (Schwab the Jew). Le Fevre had deposited linen cloth with Schwab as collateral for the loan. At the time, Abraham was living in Paris, at L'hôtel St Malo rue Beaubourg.[18] The file states that Le Fevre was swindled out of her goods and forced to pay interest on a loan, claiming that Abraham would not give her the linens he had promised.[19] According to the file, he lent her a sum of money for which he received linens as collateral. Abraham took the cotton canvas and muslin as a deposit and collateral on the loan and set an interest rate. He was to return the merchandise when Le Fevre was ready to pay back part of the sum plus interest.[20] The official complaint stated that Le Fevre did not have the 800 livres agreed upon to retrieve her linens, and that Schwab offered to accept a reduced initial amount of 500 livres with the remainder to be paid with interest. Le Fevre returned slightly short of 500 livres with 498 livres, and Schwab refused to return her goods until at least 500 livres of the initial sum was paid. Later. Le Fevre claimed that Schwab was acting in bad faith, as he had already sold her cloth and pocketed the proceeds.[21]

The next document in the file explains the story a bit differently, giving a detailed description of the alleged actions of the accused.[22] Le Fevre complained that Schwab's actions were improper and that "this was the ways Jews do business." Schwab proposed to Le Fevre that he would restore half of her goods if she were to pay back the sum that was lent, 498 livres. Le Fevre then filed her complaint, claiming that she returned the 498 pounds, but Schwab failed to restore her goods. All witnesses interviewed testified that Abraham had sold the sheets and drapes long before, and that Le Fevre had legal recourse to prosecute him in a court of law as he had stolen from her. This testimony is handwritten and addressed to the chief of police, Hérault. There are then a few letters back and forth in the file, and ultimately an order (*un placet*) to arrest "*Abraham Schwabe juif de Metz*" and place him in the prison of Châtelet by order of the king. A letter of support came from Jacob of Worms to the chief of police asking for Abraham's release, yet he remained incarcerated for a long time. After being himself accused of financial fraud, Jacob of Worms fled to Holland.[23] The authorities then sent Abraham to Bicêtre with another Jew, Nathan of Morhange.

Bautry was an official "Jew-finder". Besides Berryer, there was Langlade, a special police appointee (possibly with legal training). According to Kahn's research, he was a known anti-semite who claimed he would find a way to destroy the Schwab family, and wanted to begin deporting them.[24] Langlade authored the documents that helped to continue Abraham's testimonial letters, saying that he, Langlade, had the honor of representing many Jews in Paris, and that these Jews from Metz had certain residence certificates that served as passports allowing them to live and work in Paris. Against the wishes of Berryer, he stated that Jews from Metz should not be punished for the notorious acts of one Jew and that the court should respect the king's passports issued to the Jews of Metz, allowing them to travel freely and practice their trade. He also said that Abraham was falsely accused by the laundress, or *lingère*. It appears there are three letters of this sort in the file.[25] Langlade conducted another interview with Schwab and wrote his interpretation of the story. Schwab reported that he never lent money to Le Fevre.[26]

Whatever the truth of the matter, the context is relevant to the case of Glucka-Angélique Schwab for one important reason: Nathan de Morhange was convinced that a way out of his own predicament (prison, antisemitism, and being precluded from all aspects of work in France) was to convert to Catholicism. Abraham—the brother of Glucka-Angélique—was witness to this conversion in September 1729. Nathan de Morhange, who had been trading and working with Abraham Schwab, then stayed in the same cell as Abraham from October to November 1729. Nathan had therefore been converted to Catholicism by the musketeers and chevaliers of the king while he was still in prison. Langlade was furious and decried the act, claiming that Morhange was a great opportunist. According to Kahn, "he was converted by the comptroller and the musketeers and the king's knights."[27]

Nathan and Abraham were then sent together from Châtelet to Bicêtre in late 1729.[28] "Nathan of Morhange the other Jew, the 'so-called' Schouabe said that it was true that he agreed to hold 970 livres worth of fabric and that he paid after receiving the receipt from her."[29] Abraham repeated the refrain that he was not guilty, and Langlade continued to represent him as a big troublemaker. Nathan was mentioned for the first time in the interview brief here, in which he announced he was converting to Catholicism. In this letter, Langlade refers to Morhange by name implicates him as a co-conspirator.

> I spoke to this Jew this morning and he said he never lent money to the laundress and consequently does not have the 60 pounds of interest nor the 2853 (measurement) of the merchandise and manifestly did not take anything from her and that she tried the same thing with Nathan de Morhange...the so-called Schwab said to me that it is true that he accepted a sum of 960 pounds worth of material from this laundress that he paid following the receipt that she showed to him. I dare to assure you that this laundress that this young man is a true troublemaker, and a frequenter of whorehouses, and a gambler, and that this laundress has much to complain about...this 28th of September 1729.[30]

As such, this is where we first see the possibility of a connection to Angélique's case. It is possible that she may have heard about Nathan's conversion from her brother. Perhaps she could have chosen conversion as a potential way out of her own predicament: betrothal to a man she did not desire to marry.

The news of Jacob of Worm's (son of Joseph) imprisonment also confirms the conversion of Nathan of Morhange.[31] This letter attests to the police's sentiment towards the Jews, and it appears that Langlade, who had earlier claimed to represent Morhange and Jacob of Worms, was actively participating in efforts to rid Paris of his Jewish clients. Langlade wrote to the authorities:

> *J'ay en l'honneur de vous faire réponse le 22 mois passe a vu un placet et ma lettre de Jacob de Worms aussi juif et prisonnier au grand Chatelet vous avait écrit et marque que ce juif, et Nathan de Morhange n'exerçaient aucune religion, et insultaient tout le monde dans cette prison. Je m'en suis informe et l'on ma assure que cela était vrai, je vous proposais sur votre bon plaisir Monsieur de mettre ces deux juifs a Bicêtre, et j'ose vous assurer Monsieur avec vérité si quelqu'un a mérite d'être renfermée ce soit ces deux juifs la, le dit Schouabe, son père*

et mère et tout sa famille à Paris depuis dix ou douze ans vous m'avez donne un ordre en date ou dix-huit janvier de tolérer pendant deux mois ce juif a Paris, quoique ce temps soit échec depuis le dix-huit mars quelque chose j'ay pas pu luy dire, il ne veut pas se retirer, ce juif est frère de Jacob Schouabe qui a fait cette grosse banqueroute et qui a passé en Hollande, j'ai eu l'honneur de présenter plusieurs fois à Monsieur que tous les juifs de tels pais qu'ils puissent être sont très suspects à Paris, ceux de Metz viennent avec des certificats Monsieur Dangervilleirs leur délivre des passeports du Roy sur lequels passeports l'est expliqués qu'ils seront rapportés devant vous sous peine de nullité… .afin que monsieur y mette son vue. …

Ce 17e juillet Langlade.

I have had the honor of replying to you the 22nd of these past months and to have placed a *placet* [request] and a letter about Jacob of Worms, also a prisoner in Châtelet, I had written you and remarked that this Jew and Nathan of Morhange did not practice any religion, and that they insulted everybody in the prison. I asked around and I can assure you that this is true, I can propose to you, that we should therefore place these two Jews in Bicêtre, and I dare to assure you Monsieur in truth if anyone deserves to be thrown into prison it is these two Jews, the "so-called" Schouabe, his father and his mother and all of his family are in Paris for ten to twelve years and you have given me an order with the date of the 18 of January to tolerate their presence. It is two months that this Jew is in Paris and there seems to be a stalling of the process, and something I cannot tell what? He does not want to go away, and this Jew is the brother of the famous Jacob Schouab who did the famous financial fraud and who escaped to Holland, I had the honor of presenting all these Jews many times to Monsieur, whatever country they are in…they are always very suspect in Paris. Those who are in Paris have certificates from Monsieur Dangevilliers who delivers them the passports from the king…and these passports are supposed to bring them under your control…

17th July Langlade.[32]

This story presents a complicated intrigue, and making sense of it necessitates a degree of speculation. Considering all the facts

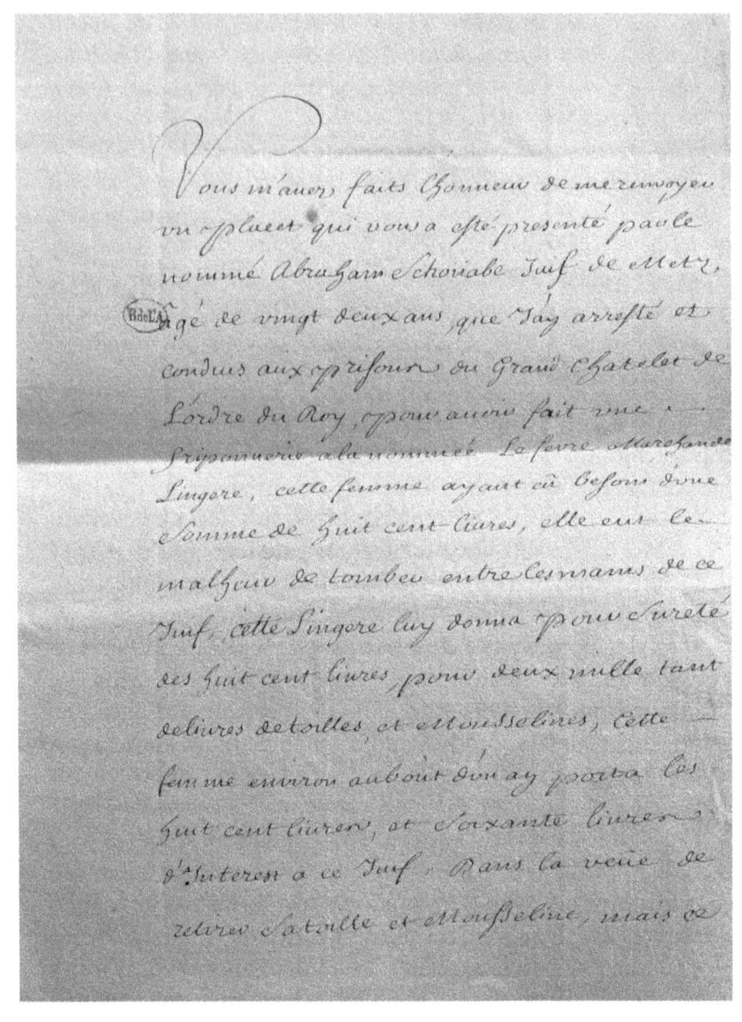

Vous m'avez faits l'honneur de me renvoyer
un placet qui vous a esté presenté par le
nommé Abraham Schwabe Juif de Metz,
âgé de vingt deux ans, que j'ay arresté et
conduis aux prisons du Grand Chatelet de
l'ordre du Roy, pour avoir fait une
friponnerie a la nommée Lefevre Marchande
Lingere, cette femme ayant eu besoin d'une
somme de huit cent livres, elle eut le
malheur de tomber entre les mains de ce
Juif, cette Lingere luy donna pour sureté
des huit cent livres, pour deux mille tant
de livres de toilles, et mousselines, cette
femme environ au bout d'un an porta les
huit cent livres, et soixante livres
d'interest a ce Juif, dans la veue de
retirer sa toille et mousseline, mais ce

Figure 5.1 Page one of letter from Langlade for the record. Photograph by the author.

Source: AN, LL 1641, 4.

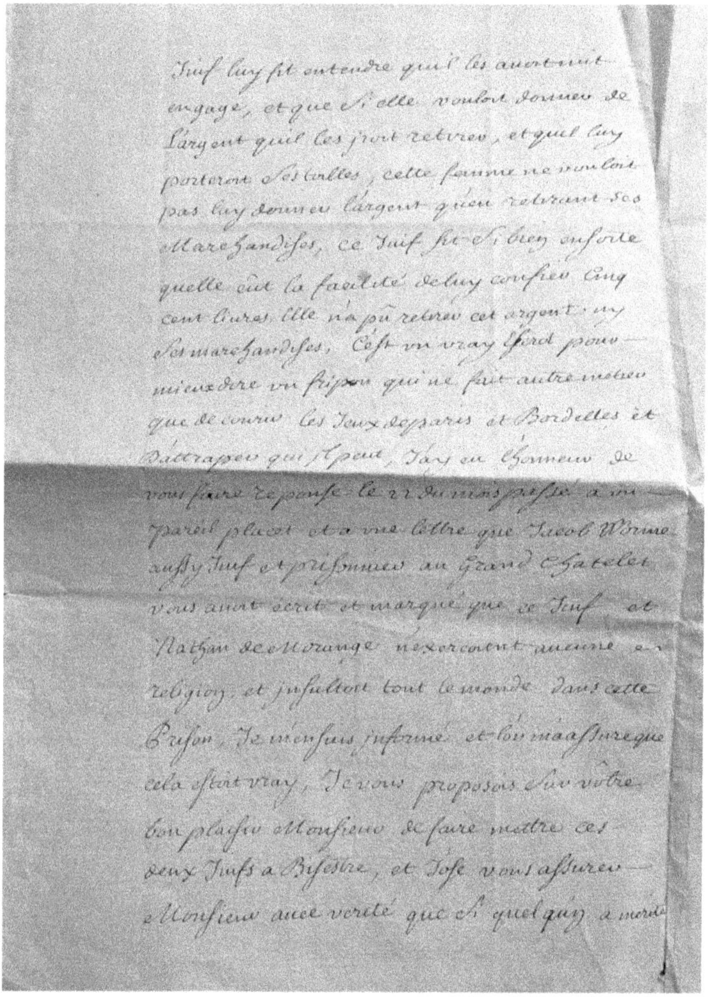

Juif luy fit entendre qu'il les avoit mit engagé, et que si elle vouloit donner de l'argent qu'il les iroit retirer, et qu'il luy porteroit ses toilles, cette femme ne vouloit pas luy donner l'argent qu'en retirant ses Marchandises, ce Juif fit si bien enforte qu'elle eut la facilité de luy confier cinq cent livres. Elle n'a pû retirer cet argent, ny ses marchandises, C'est un vray effrond pour mieux dire un fripon qui ne fait autre metier que de courir les Jeux de hazards et Bordelles et d'attraper qui il peut, J'ay eu l'honneur de vous faire reponse le 22 du mois passé a un pareil placet et a une lettre que Jacob Worms aussy Juif et prisonnier au Grand Chatelet vous avoit écrit et marqué que ce Juif et Nathan de Morange n'exercoient aucune religion, et insultoit tout le monde dans cette Prison, Je m'en suis informé et l'on m'a assuré que cela estoit vray, Je vous proposois sur votre bon plaisir Monsieur de faire mettre ces deux Juifs a Bicestre, et J'ose vous assurer Monsieur avec verité que si quelqu'un a merité

Figure 5.2 Page two of letter from Langlade for the record. Photograph by the author.

Source: AN, LL 1641, 4.

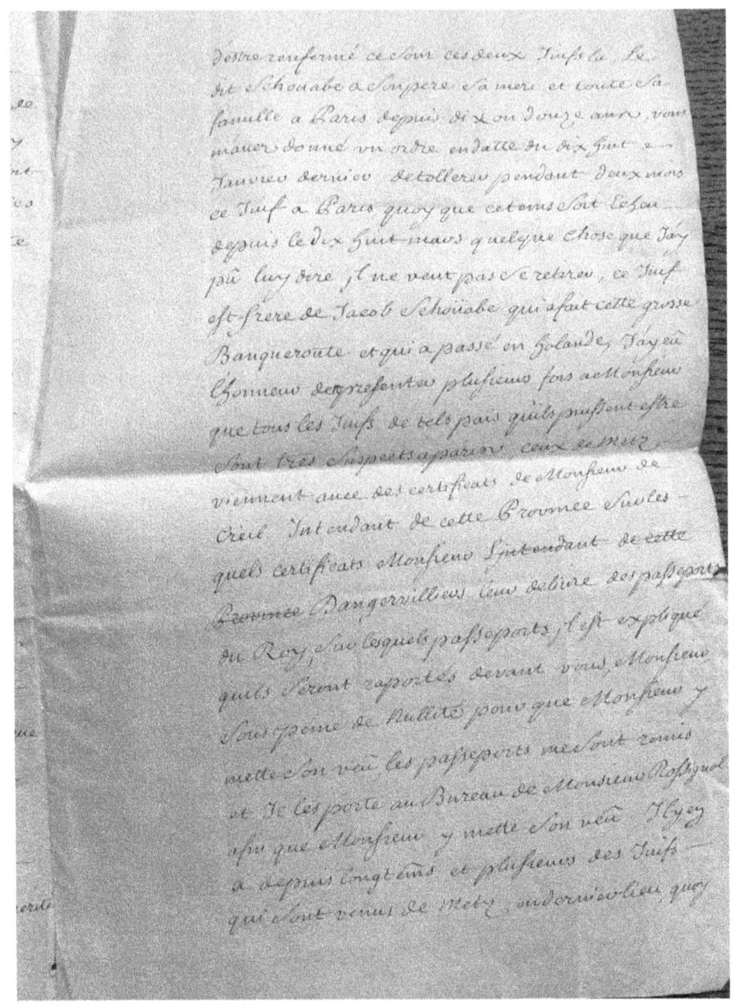
d'estre renfermé ce sont ces deux Juifs le, le
dit Schouabe a [illegible] sa mere et toute sa
famille a Paris depuis dix ou douze ans, vous
m'avez donné un ordre en datte du dix huit e
Janvier dernier de tollerer pendant deux mois
ce Juif a Paris quoy que ce tems soit Escou
depuis le dix huit mars quelque chose que j'ay
pû luy dire, il ne veut pas se retirer, ce Juif
est frere de Jacob Schouabe qui a fait cette grosse
Banqueroute et qui a passé en holande, J'ay eu
l'honneur de representer plusieurs fois a Monsieur
que tous les Juifs de tels pais qu'ils puissent estre
sont tres suspects a paris, ceux de Metz
viennent avec des certifficats de Monsieur de
Creil Intendant de cette Province sur lesquels certifficats Monsieur l'intendant de cette
Province Dangervilliers leur delivre des passeports
du Roy, sur lesquels passeports, il est expliqué
qu'ils seront raportés devant vous, Monsieur
sous peine de nullité pour que Monsieur y
mette son veu, les passeports me sont remis
et Je les porte au Bureau de Monsieur Rossignol
afin que Monsieur y mette son veü. Il y en
a depuis longtems et plusieurs des Juifs
qui sont venus de Metz, ou [illegible] quoy

Figure 5.3 Page three of letter from Langlade for the record. Photograph by the author.

Source: AN, LL 1641, 5.

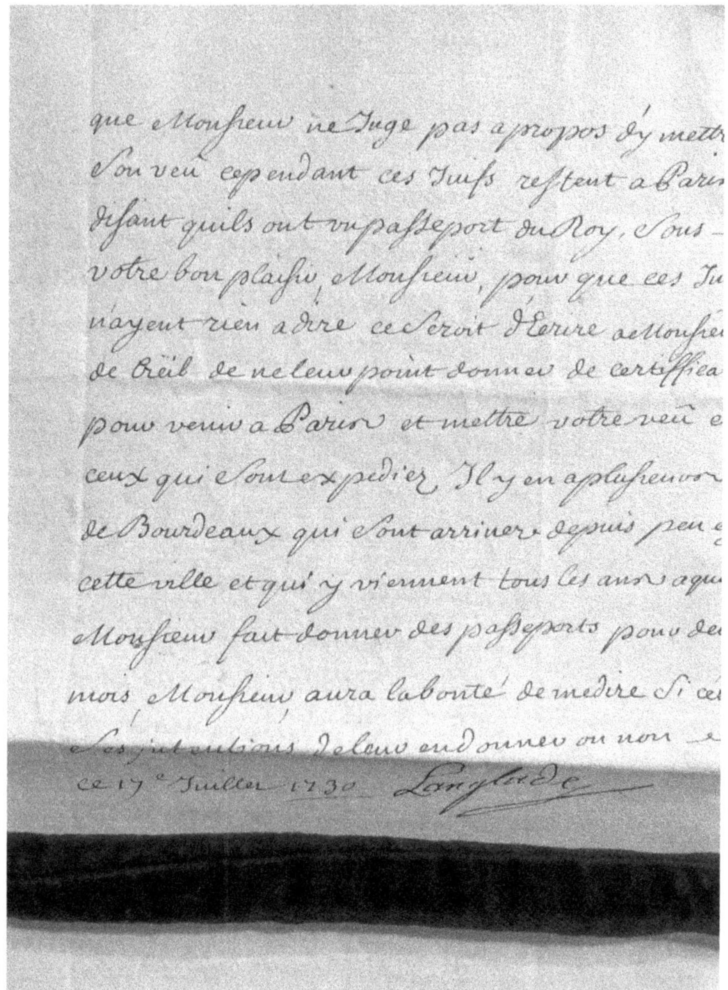

que Monsieur ne Juge pas apropos dy mett
son veu cependant ces Juifs restent a Paris
disant quils ont un passeport du Roy, sous
votre bon plaisir, Monsieur, pour que ces Ju
nayent rien adire ce seroit d'Ecrire a Monsie
de Breil de ne leur point donner de certiffica
pour venir a Paris et mettre votre veu e
ceux qui sont expediez Il y en a plusieurs
de Bourdeaux qui sont arrivez depuis peu e
cette ville et qui y viennent tous les ans a qu
Monsieur fait donner des passeports pour de
mois Monsieur aura la bonte de me dire si ce
ses intentions de leur en donner ou non
ce 17e Juillet 1730 Langlade

Figure 5.4 Page four of letter from Langlade for the record. Photograph by the author.

Source: AN, LL 1641, 5.

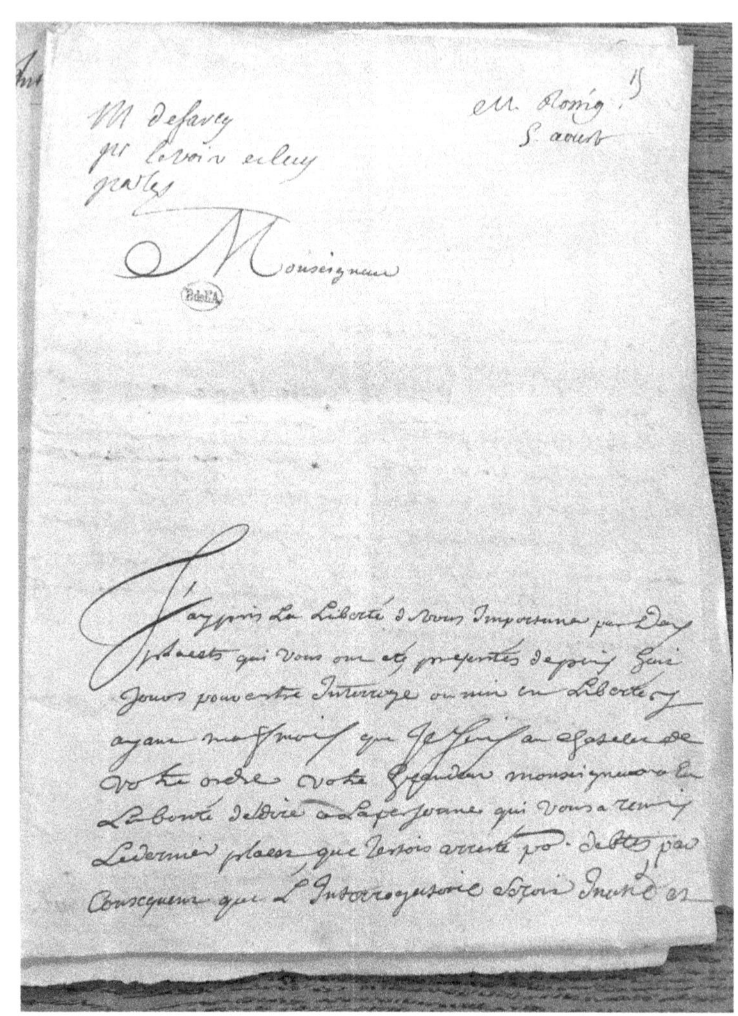

Monseigneur

J'ay pris La Liberté d vous Importuner par Deux placets qui vous ont eté presentés depuis Seize Jours pour estre Interrogé ou mis en Liberté y ayant neuf mois que Je suis au chastelet de Votre ordre Votre Grandeur monseigneur a eu La bonté de dire a La personne qui vous a remis Le dernier placet que J'estois arresté po. dettes par Consequent que L'Interrogatoire estoit Inutile et

Figure 5.5 Page one of letter from Abraham Schwab to De Farcy. Photograph by the author.

Source: AN, LL 1641, 5.

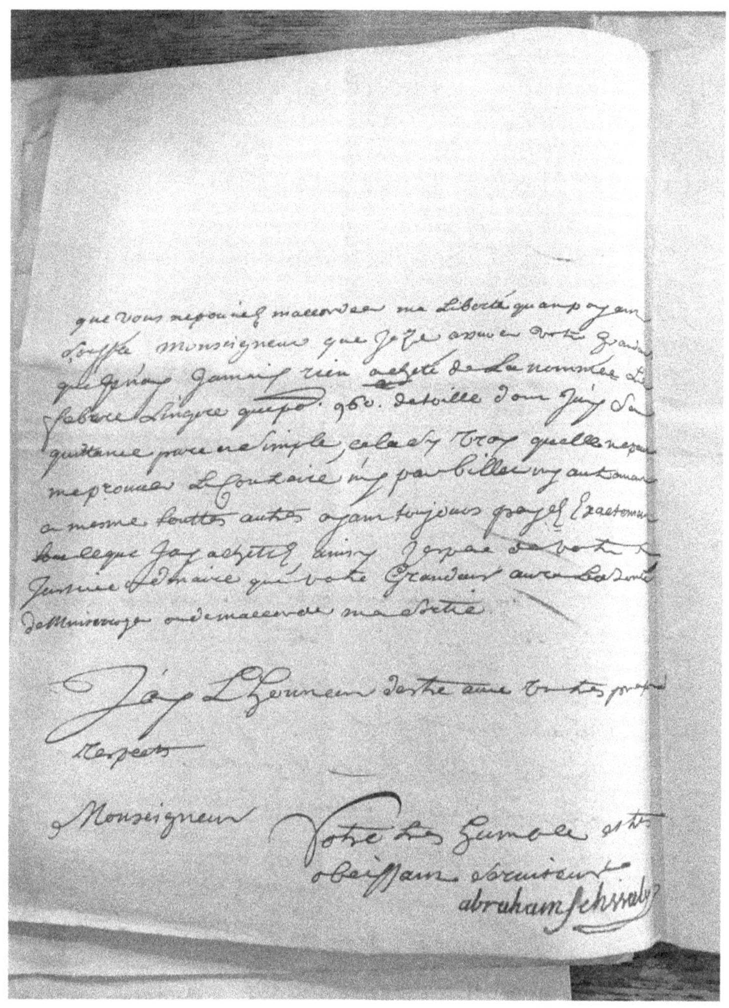

que vous ne pouviez m'accorder ma liberté qu'en payant
souffre Monseigneur que je le assure votre Grandeur
que je n'ay jamais rien acheté de la nommée Le
febvre Lingère que pour 960. de toille dont j'ay sa
quittance par une simple, cela est vray qu'elle ne peut
me prouver le contraire ny par billet ny autrement
a mesme toutes autres ayant toujours payé exactement
[illegible] ce que j'ay acheté ainsy j'espère de votre
justice et débonnaire que votre Grandeur aura la bonté
de [illegible] ou de m'accorder ma sortie.

J'ay l'honneur d'estre avec toutes profond
respects

Monseigneur

Votre très humble et très
obeissant serviteur
abraham Schwab

Figure 5.6 Page two of letter from Abraham Schwab to De Farcy. Photograph by the author.

Source: AN, LL 1641, 5.

of the case, I believe there is another very interesting aspect of this story to uncover. At the end of Abraham's file, he was finally remanded and released. His release was put off for some time, and he wrote two letters to De Farcy about the lack of communication and was then informed of his release. There is also a second letter for Abraham's release, as the first *mise en liberté*, or "release form" was rejected. This letter is the second request for a release.[33]

> *Abraham Schoaube*
> *Magistrat de Farcy*
> *5 aout*
> *Addresse illisible*
> *Monseigneur,*
> *J'ai pris la liberté de vous importuner par dire que les placets qui vous ont été présents depuis quelques jours pour être interrogée ou mis en liberté y ayant neuf mois que je suis au châtelet [prison] de votre ordre votre grandeur Monseigneur en liberté de dire à la préférence qui vous a remis le dernier placet que je sois arrêté pour dettes par conséquences que l'interrogatoire je crois inane et que vous ne pouvez m'accorde ma liberté quand ayant souffert Monseigneur que je ne vous assure votre grandeur quelques jamais rien acheté de la nommée Le Fevre Lingère [illisible] [pris pour?] 960 livres de toiles. 2 ans J'ai fait la quittance parce que simple cela sy trop elle ne peut pas prouver la notaire ny par billet ny au jamais ce même toutes autres y a toujours payer exactement tout ce que j'ai acheté, amis et j'espère de votre …justice et avis que votre grandeur avec la bonté de Monseigneur…m'accord a liberté.*
> *J'ay l'honneur d'être avec votre profond respect,*
> *Monseigneur,*
> *Votre humble et obéissant serviteur,*
> *Abraham Schwab.*

I have taken the liberty to inconvenience you by saying that the "petitions" or "placets" that were presented to you a few days ago to be investigated, or to be set free have been tabled for nine months and I have been in Chatêlet prison under your order grand Monseigneur. You are at liberty to say according to your preference whether or not I should be arrested or for debts and consequentially the interrogation,

I think to be inane and that you could accord me my liberty and that I have indeed suffered Monsieur, I assure you I did not buy anything from the named "Le Fevre Laundress" nor did I take 960 pounds from her. I gave her an exception because simply put she could not notarize what was owed, even though others have been able to do that exactly, pay exactly what I owed. I hope that your Justice and good opinion will give me liberty.

Monseigneur,
With honor and profound respect,
Your humble and obedient servant,
Abraham Schwab.[34]

Abraham wrote two letters before his release was affected. The above is the second letter. His departure from prison was delayed for nine months while the magistrate reviewed his release forms. One might speculate that the release form sat on the desk of Berryer, the rabidly antisemitic police chief, until he was compelled by the king to act on it. This following transcription is an excerpt from the letter from Rossignol, a lawyer, and written for the record of his release. This is an excerpt from the last document in the dossier of Abraham Schwab:

Ce Raisonnement ne signifie pas qu'elle lui a confié une somme, c'est cependant, Monseigneur ce qu'elle a insinué à votre grandeur avec artifice…

Toutes dépositions contraires aux énonciations que la dite Schwabe…

C'est un préjugé bien favorable pour luy…déterminerons Votre Grandeur à luy accorder sa liberté.

Il ne cessera de faire des vœux pour la conservation de votre illustre majesté.

This reasoning does not signify that she gave him a sum, it is therefore Monseigneur to your greatness that she insinuated an artifice…All the depositions to the contrary and denunciation of the so-called Schwab and prejudiced and therefore favorable for him…Let us determine to give him his liberty. We continue to offer our best wishes for your illustrious majesty.[35] [Full record transcribed in endnote.]

Glucka-Angélique

Angélique Schwab converted from Judaism to Catholicism in the fall of 1729. Her file appears in the subsequent pages after that of Abraham Schwab in a file labeled "*juifs*," or "Jews," in the Bastille Archives.[36] She converted during her claustration, and her "*ordre du roi*" mentions that she made several pleas to become Catholic. In studying her file, I have found various accounts of stories that the factum and her personal documents tell, which are also corroborated by notes in the Archives Israelites, the Jewish communal records. In the records of the Archives Israelites, she was first recorded under her Yiddish name, Glucka.[37] Glucka-Angélique's father, Ruben de Metz (Jews were often referred to by their place of origin rather than surname, as in "de Metz" instead of "Schwab"), was a banker and had selected a good, traditional match for his daughter. Glucka would receive a generous 500 livres "*de patrimoine*."

As a Jewish woman by birth, Glucka was accorded very limited agency. In the act of converting, she superseded her father's authority. It also appears that she first refused to marry a man to whom she was betrothed. Her "fiancé" was in London when she turned eighteen years of age in 1729. Leon Kahn proposes that she may have met a Catholic man who convinced her to convert for love. In a series of mysterious events between September and October of 1729, Glucka somehow met with priests in a *Maison de Conversion*. According to Kahn, she was interviewed by several priests and decided to convert to Catholicism. Apparently, she had many conversations with "*différents catholiques*" (different Catholics) and even with priests. In the records we learn that she left her father, mother, brother, and sister, abandoned her wealth, and asked the king for a pension for her conversion. It also appears that she may have been given a third name in the convent, as "Olique" appears in her records later in the Convent de la Providence.[38]

Schwab was from a wealthy Jewish family from Metz. Her father, Ruben Schwab, had arranged a brilliant future for her. He had made it clear that he would give her everything that could make her happy. As was the custom, he settled her betrothal to a Jewish man from a good family in London.[39] So why did Glucka Schwab protest her family's tradition of betrothal? This tradition of matchmaking was an accepted way of life for Jews throughout the world in the eighteenth century (and it remains so for many highly religious Jews). In his account of Glucka-Angélique's conversion, Kahn poses a question that suggests a sort of "mutinous" activity against her father: "Were these mutinous acts pointedly against her father's will?" Betrothal is a religious custom that holds a sacred trust in patriarchal authority. Kahn asks, "Why would she want to rupture the most sacred of connections?"; "What good is it to protest the father's authority, when the highest authority to address is the king's authority?"[40] The extension of the paternal authority of the father to the highest patriarchal authority of the king is brought into question, when the daughter Glucka can bypass her father's authority in order to petition the king.

In seeking to understand Glucka's choices, it is important to note that the Nouvelles Catholiques was a convent especially dedicated to the conversion of young women, usually those converting from Judaism or Protestantism. It seems that they had a particular interest in receiving Jewish girls, as Kahn has established in his study of the legal records of the Bastille.[41] The Nouvelles Catholiques building is no longer in existence, though it used to be located on the rue Saint-Anne (almost directly opposite the current entrance of the Bibliothèque Richelieu).[42] Generally, Jews who converted to Christianity did so to improve their station, and because of the extreme societal prejudice against them. What makes the situation of Angélique Schwab so unusual is that at the time Jewish women rarely converted. We suspect that the path to the convent may not have been often chosen by Jewish women for many reasons, among them that patrilocal and religious rule afforded Jewish women very little unsupervised contact with the gentile public.[43]

Some Protestant women entered the Nouvelles Catholiques by requesting *ordres du roi* (orders from the king), and there are more than a few requests that seem motivated by a sincere desire to convert to Catholicism. There were other important benefits to securing entrance to the community as well, not least of which was access to food and shelter and the possibility of finding an apprenticeship or even seeding a dowry through charitable donations. The records of Glucka-Angelique's entry into the convent and conversion offer some insight into her decisions. The only archival documentation on file other than the *lettre de cachet* in her legal brief is the written documentation of her entry the Convent of the Nouvelles Catholiques.[44]

When considering the reasons Angélique might have gone to such extremes to leave her community, Leon Kahn offers some insights. It may be that there was a combination of causes:

1. Abraham was in prison with Nathan of Morhange and could have communicated that conversion was a good idea.
2. She really was attracted to the faith, but it is very unclear how she would become exposed in the first place.
3. She had met and fallen in love with a Catholic man, though again, how she would be exposed to this possibility is a big question.
4. She sought out pathways to block her father's authority and the match that was awaiting her.

Here Kahn recounts some of Angélique's testimony:

> At first, she was attracted as she had said, to the discourse of different Catholics, even the priests that they had presented to her. She leaned definitively in this direction especially towards the brilliant truths that the vicar of the parish of St Jean, M. Valerot, who is charged with religious education, he opened her eyes.[45]

We can also locate documentation from October 1729 of a conversation that Langlade had with Angélique, during which she insisted on converting from Judaism to Catholicism. Glucka is called Angélique in all the legal briefs from October 1729, and there is no reference to her Jewish name after this point. According to Langlade, "She is a very reasonable young women, her face is charming enough, and is what we could call well spoken."[46] Kahn reports:

> Langlade was moved by the desolation of this child and by her desperate determination. She inspired in him much more interest than she should have for simply fleeing the "English Jew." Especially because she demonstrated a deep desire to be Catholic, who did not want to marry, but be baptized instead. They made her sign the conversion form which she signed in

> Hebrew and in English: "I the undersigned from my pure and proper will without being forced by any human, but from a true desire to embrace the Christian religion, do in the matter of this subject present a request to Monsieur the lieutenant of police, in faith of which I sign the present protestation to attach to my conversion form, done in Paris 29 of September, 1729."[47]

In her petition, Angélique expressed her desire to convert to Catholicism but explained that doing so would require her to sever ties with her family and abandon her 500-livre inheritance. Since she claimed to have no trade by which she could support herself, she asked the police to help her enter a community and provide a pension *viagère* (a stipend for a non-permanent resident) that would enable her to subsist after her conversion. This request was granted.

The following *placet* (petition) (Figure 5.7) presents the story of Angélique Schwab in a very different light:

> *Angélique Ruben Schouabe âgée de dix-huit ans, fille de Ruben Schouab, Banquier Juif, s'étant trouvée plusieurs fois avec différentes Catholiques, mêmes avec des prêtres dont le discours l'ont entièrement déterminé à quitter sa religion pour embrasser la Religion Chrétienne, être baptisée et en remplir le mieux qu'elle pourra toutes les fonctions comme pour être généreuse et louable entreprise il faut qu'elle quitte père et mère, frère, sœur, et toute sa famille avec au moins cinq mille livres de patrimoine qu'elle a espéré qu'un d'un cote elle ne possède aucun talent pour vivre par elle-même, que de plus pour être instruite de notre religion, il est absolument nécessaire qu'elle soit mise dans une communauté, dans laquelle "M" Valerot, vicaire de la Paroisse St. Jean qui s'est bien voulu charger de cette instruction puisse facilement y apporter ses soin(g)s, la ditte Angélique Ruben Schouab, Shorat) sur le rapport qui lui a été fait de notre probité, et du parfait amour que vous avez pour notre religion a créé le plus sûr moyen de venir à bout de son dessin, était de s'adresser à Notre Grandeur pour lui procurer entrée dans une communauté pour après y avoir après tous les devoirs de notre religion, être baptisée et avoir Parain, et Marraine, qu'elle espère que vous voudriez bien luy choisir elle se flatte aussi par votre crédit, elle pourra obtenir*

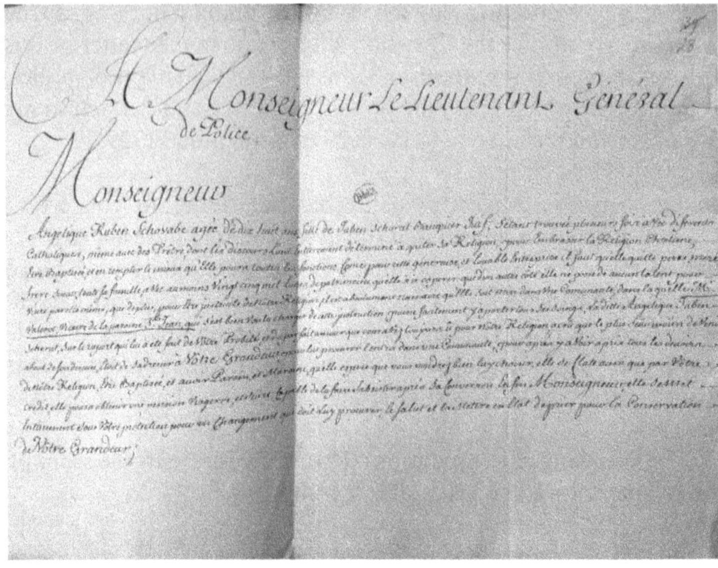

A Monseigneur le Lieutenant Général de Police

Monseigneur

Figure 5.7 The *lettre de cachet* or petition of the king granting permission for Angélique to convert. This petition had the power to overrule her father's command to marry within her faith. Photograph by the author.

Source: AB, MS 11072, 28.

une pension viagère et sécure capable de la faire subsister après sa conversion. Enfin Monseigneur, elle se met entièrement sous votre protection pour vu changement qui lui procurer le fallut et la mettre en état de prier pour la conservation de notre grandeur.

Angélique Ruben Schwab: aged 18 years, daughter of the Jewish banker Ruben Schwab, having been found many times among different Catholics, even with priests, of whom the discourse had externally determined that she should leave her religion, to embrace the Christian Faith. To be baptized and to fulfill to the best of her ability and so that she may function and for this generous and praiseworthy enterprise, she must leave her father and mother, brother, and sister all her family with at least 25,000 livres of patrimony which she hopes will help her sustain a modest lifestyle. She possesses no talent to live on her own, and more and more finds that being instructed in our religion, it is necessary for her to be put into a community in which M. Le Vicaire Valerot, Vicar of the Parish of St. Jean who was well charged with this instruction, can easily take care of all her needs. The so-called Angélique Ruben Schwab, under the report that was already made under your incorruptible scrutiny and for the love that you have for our religion, have thought that there are many ways to come to "His Design," one way is to address ourselves to "His Greatness" in order to procure entry into our community, and to prove after having aspired to all the work of our religion, to be baptized, to have Godfather and Godmother, that she hopes that you will choose for her, she would grateful if you would honor/merit/accord her a travel pension that would also allow her to subsist after her conversion. Finally, Monseigneur, that she should be entirely under your protection for a change that should be procured for her, it is necessary to put her in the hands of the State, and to pray for the Conservation of your Grandeur.[48]

The sisters in the convents kept a record of every girl who entered the community (voluntarily or not) after 1704. Angélique appears in the first entry to the Nouvelles Catholiques as Olique Schouabe, and shortly thereafter when she was baptized. The register states that she was eighteen and came from Metz, and it lists the names of her parents. She was baptized in May 1731 in the Nouvelles Catholiques community and left a year later to enter the Couvent de la Providence in Paris. According to the records, it seems she adopted the name Marie Louise Adelaide after her baptism and left *Nouvelles Catholiques* in August 1732, "after having been wisely directed the receiving sacraments of penitence, confirmation and the Eucharist."[49] A marginal note suggests that she experienced a health crisis while in the community, as it says that she was baptized in May 1731 by the bishop of Puy while in her bed. This likely would have been done only if she had been near death (Figure 5.8).[50]

Angélique was probably refused a dowry by her father and may have instead received a pension from the king for her conversion and maintenance. Haley Bowen says in her research of Angélique

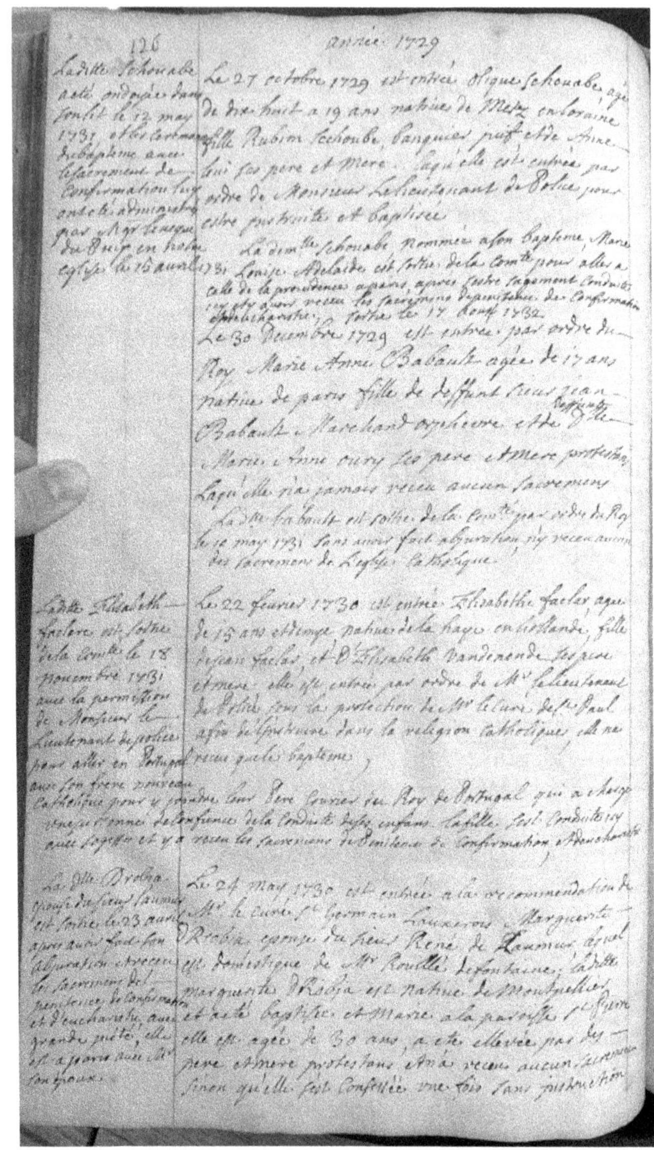

Figure 5.8 . Baptism record of Angélique at the Couvent de la Providence in Paris. Photograph by Haley Bowen.

Source: AN, LL 1642, 126.

Schwab, "Due to name changes, it is difficult to find religious women in this context—she may have entered as a lay pensioner, in which case she would have retained her new name, or she may have received yet another new name if she entered as a nun or converse sister."[51]

According to the records, Angélique succeeded against all odds to free herself from patriarchal control of her religion, community, and family. She gained the sympathy of several religious Catholics, the police, and finally the king. She managed to catalyze the overruling of her father's betrothal to a man she did not love. She entered the convent, lived there for a year, but was moved to a hospice type of convent, and there the record ends.

In summary, patrilocal authority was prevalent in all Jewish communities in Western Europe during the eighteenth century. The King of France allowed the Jews, and especially the fathers and rabbis, to govern their own people for the most part. As can be seen in the case of Glucka-Angélique Schwab, patriarchal authority in the Jewish community was left to rabbinical control, and the rabbi was beholden to the king's control. Fathers and men in the Jewish community executed religiously controlled governance but also acted in accordance with the king's rulings. Since the king approved the rabbis as community leaders, he left matters in the hands of his personally approved community leaders. This was a form of indirect governance and helped maintain the patriarchal order of his subjects. We can trace a line from the king's authority to the Jewish community and thus Glucka's father. I conclude that by converting to Catholicism, Angélique was resisting patriarchal authority.

Angélique was baptized in her bed (presumably during an illness, since most girls in the register with this note tend to die soon afterwards) on 12 May 1731, and this information was confirmed by the Bishop of Puy in April of the same year. In August 1732, she seems to have left the convent of Nouvelles Catholiques for the Couvent de la Providence in Paris, so she did not remain there for the better part of her life afterwards, and circumstances, probably an illness, had her transferred to the Couvent de la Providence. This is where the record, the story, and probably the life of Angélique Schwab, née Glucka, end. Paradoxically, in this case, the king helped her escape her filial obligations, but it seems Glucka's resistance ultimately proved fatal.

Notes

1 See Chapter 2 for a deeper discussion of this issue.

2 Recently I overheard a tour guide in Paris on the rue des Rosiers refer to this section of the Marais as the Jewish ghetto.

3 See Arthur Hertzberg. *The French Enlightenment and the Jews* (New York: Columbia University Press, 1968), 84.

4 The 1215 Magna Carta of England, which famously placed limitations on the ability of the monarch to collect debts in favor of the rebel barons, is widely seen as an advance in the creation of democratic norms. That same document limited the ability of Jewish bankers to collect debts owed by the barons. Jewish bankers served a vital role in financing royal enterprises and were associated with the power of the monarchy while attracting the ire of the general population. These attitudes remained in place across Europe throughout the centuries. We see in the case of these Jewish bankers in Paris that they were under the protection of the king while resented by the populace.

5 Leon Kahn, *Les Juifs de Paris au Dix-Huitième Siècle: d'après les archives de la lieutenance générale de la police à la Bastille* (Paris: Darlucher, 1894), 38.

6 According to Frances Malino, "The '*Lettres Patentes*' also helped to maintain discipline within the community, the syndics had at their disposal a multitude of fines, and for the most extreme cases which included bringing complaints against fellow Jews to non-Jewish authorities or courts excommunication. This deprived the guilty of the services of the community and of all relations, even commerce, with co-religionists." "Resistance and Rebellion in Eighteenth-Century France," *Jewish Historical Studies* 30 (1987): 56.

7 Kahn, *Juifs de Paris*, i. "Jews were numerous suspects." All translations by the author unless otherwise stated.

8 Kahn says that Jacob of Worms was the exception, as it seems he did not need a passport since he was not only an important banker but also an arms dealer for the king since 1700. Ibid., 39.

9 "*Juifs qui sont à Paris sans passeport et méritent d'être chassez pour être trouvé sans passeport…Nathan Schowabe. Dit estre entre process contre Saloman Schowabe.*" Ibid., 6.

10 "*Les femmes n'étaient guère plus épargnées. Tous étaient des gens qu'il fallait exiler, 'des mauvais sujets' dont il était bon de purger Paris.*" Ibid., 25.

11 It may be that Glucka was named for Gluckel of Hameln. She was an ancestor of Glucka and, and according to Hertzberg, "a woman of great piety and extraordinary business acumen, [she] also bemoaned the ways of the rich, but unlike Hourwitz she ascribed their sins not

to economic oppression and superstitious belief but rather to spiritual laxity. When she first arrived, she confided in later years in her memoires, Metz was a noble and pious community." Hertzberg, *French Enlightenment*, 239.

12 Geneanet, "Gluck "Angélique" Schwab," accessed 24 May 2023, https://gw.geneanet.org/alanguggenheim?lang=en&n=schwab&oc=0&p=gluck+angelique.

13 Hertzberg, *French Enlightenment*, 201.

14 Samuel Lévy was the son-in-law of the well-known Glucka of Hamlin. Ibid., 239.

15 Paris, Archives de la Bastille (AB), MS 11072, 4.

16 In 1721, Elie Schwab, of the same family as Samuel Lévy, became rabbi in Haguenau through family influence. He received formal recognition that year from Louis XV as rabbi of all of Lower Alsace. Hertzberg, *French Enlightenment*, 239.

17 This is the passage in French that has been summarized: *Schouabe, Abraham à Monsieur Hérault Lieutenant général de police.* "*Monsieur: Marie le Fevre, marchande lingère à Paris représente très humblement, à Votre Grandeur qu'ayant besoin de 800 livres pour faire honneur à quelques lettres d'échange ou lui indique le nomme "Chouabe juif" de présent à Paris à l'hôtel St Malo rue Beaubourg. Ce juif preta á la représentante la somme de 800 livres moyennant 160 livres d'intérêt pour un an, il prit en nantissement pour 2853 livres de merchandise de toute mousseline que la représentante lui mit en mains sans en tirer de reconnaissance croyant ce juif de bonne foi.*" AB, MS 11072, 4.

18 The Jews of Metz lived in the third arrondissement of Paris. "The wealthy oligarchy supplied grain and horses to the government, as well as much-needed credit; the poor found themselves peddling used clothing and lending money to non-Jews who were themselves no less poverty-stricken. It is said, however, that they also marketed a most delicious goose pâté. All resided in the Jewish quarter of the city, and only there could they own property." Hertzberg, *French Enlightenment*, 6.

19 The selling of textiles such as rags, linens, and cloths was a typical Jewish occupation in medieval times.

20 In an era before ATMs and credit cards, moneylending, a precursor to consumer credit, including pawnbroking, provided a vital service in commercial and personal economic activities. This activity was certainly looked upon with disdain, and the social tensions between a disliked banking class and a populace that feared being taken advantage of and under economic pressure were bound to erupt in accusations and criminal complaints, whether justified or not. According to the reports of this incident, Abraham went to Le Fevre's house to seize the

collateral, purchased with the funds he had extended. Schouabe asked his creditor to pay back the full sum of money plus the interest before he would give back her goods.

21 The petition is transcribed here: "*Ce juif preta à la représentante la somme de 800" moyennant 160" d'intérêt pour un an, il prit en nantissement pour 2853" de merchandise de toute mousseline que la représentante lui mit en mains sans en tirer de reconnaissance croyant ce juif de bonne foi. Au temps convenu la représentante alla dire que son argent était prêt il lui promit de lui rapporter les marchandises le jour même mais une heure après il vint chez elle lui dire qu'il fallait qu'elle lui donnât d'avance l'argent qu'il lui avait donné avec intérêt, que c'était leur usage de ne rien rapporter san cela, la représentante se tourmenta beaucoup pour ne lui rien donner qu'elle n'eut ses effets. Enfin il lui proposa qu'elle lui donnât d'abord 500": et qu'il lui rapporterait l'autre moitié de ses effets. La représentante lui donnerait les 467" restant, et qu'il rapporeroit l'autre moitié des effets. La représentante lui donner 498" mais il ne lui rapportera aucun de ses effets, et a toujours amuse de plusieurs fausses raisons. La représentante, qui voulant savoir ce qu'il avait joué les 498" espérant de gagner de quoi rendre les effets. Ce qui étant avait joué le 498 espérant de gagner de quoi rendre les effets. Ce qui étant un vol manifeste. Elle a recours Monseigneur, á l'autorité de N.N pour la supplier très humblement (attendu les preuves qu'elle offre par témoins et son livre journal) de donner vos ordres afin que le dit 'juif' soit constitué prisonnier pour qu'elle puisse recevoir son don, sans quoi elle est ruinée, et elle priera le seigneur pour la conservation de Votre Grandeur*." AB, MS 11072, 4.

22 Here is the transcribed petition: "*Le nome Chouabe juif, ordre du 28 (septembre) 1729 De Monsieur Langlade affaire duquel pour fin s'informer exactement (examen) rendre compte de septembre 1729.* "*Vous m'avez fait l'honneur de me renvoyer un placet qui vous a été présente par le nommée Marie le Fevre Marchande lingère pas lequel elle expose qu'ayant eu besoin d'argent pour payer quelques lettres d'échange, elle emprunta huit cents livres ou nomme Schouabe juif en lui payant cent soixante livres d'interférer (pouvez as. Illisible) Et que pour la valeur de cette somme de huit cents livres savoir y comprendre les interférences elle lui mit pour manifestement deux mille huit cent cinquante-trois livres*." Ibid., 5

23 Hertzberg this affair in *French Enlightenment*, 124, as well as the history of the Schwab rabbinical family, 238-239.

24 This transcription gives us a look at the verbiage of the *placet*, showing how stories were retold and shaped to anticipate a certain result: "*Abraham Schouabe juif, âgé de 22 ans représente très respectueusement a Votre Grandeur que le septembre dernier, il a été*

arrêté et constitue prisonnier aux prisons du grand Chatelet en vertu d'un ordre du Roy sur un faux expose par le nommée Le Fevre Lingère qui prétend contre toute vérité aussi confie au suppliant une somme de 500 livres quoi qu'il n'ait jamais faire aussi cette femme avec cette d'autre négociations qu'un achat de marchandises pour la somme de 960 livres. Dont elle lui a donné quittance le suppliant ignore des raisons qui ont poussé cette femme dans l'injuste procédée qu'elle tient contre lui par ses considérations. Monseigneur le suppliant a recours à la justice autorité de Votre Grandeur qu'il supplie très humblement de vouloir bien faire lever l'ordre du Roy et de le mettre en liberté sy mieux elle n'aime auparavant nomme tel commissaire qu'il vous plaire en fausses informations de la liberté, il ne cessera de faire des vœux et prières. Monseigneur, pour La prospérité De Votre Grandeur." AB, MS 11072, 10.

25 "The Schwab family was not only one of the wealthiest in Metz, but also apparently one of the most litigious. In the same year (1709), Jacob Schwab fought with his brothers and brothers-in-law over the will of their mother and mother-in-law. Dissatisfied with the rabbi's decisions, Jacob threatened to take the case beyond the community. The rabbi fined and excommunicated Jacob, who then, in turn, sought and received the support of the *procureur du roi* who summoned Rabbi Brodot before the bailliage court. The Jews were seeking to establish a 'sovereign' and 'despotic' authority, the rabbi was told, which would trouble the orderly functioning of the kingdom. The nation, through its lawyer Maître Nicolas Marc, defended its rights and accused the *procureur du roi* of preventing the Jews from freely exercising their religious obligations. The Parlement subsequently issued its arret of December 1709 protecting Jacob Schwab from any further criminal action against him. The rabbi and community leaders risked a fine of 3000 livres and a prison sentence. The following year the brothers Baruch and Mayer Weil, outraged by the behaviour of Rabbi Braude, who had given their promissory note of 6000 livres to the banker Aaron Worms, appeared before the Lieutenant-General with a request to bring both the rabbi and Worms before the bailliage court. The rabbi held the promissory note against the disappearance of the brothers." Malino, "Resistance and Rebellion," 63.

26 Note that the file of Angélique Schwab was entered into the court record on November 3, 1729. The case of Abraham Schwab was documented in September of that same year, and he was in prison by mid-October. Kahn reported that October was when Angélique requested to meet with a priest; by November 3, Angélique's formal request to enter the Convent des Nouvelles Catholiques and a petition were filed.

27 "*Il se faisait catéchiser par un contrôleur général de mousquetaires et de chevaliers de la garde du roi.*" *Juifs de Paris*, 24.

28 Here is a transcription of the original petition: "*Monsieur, Vous m'avez fait l'honneur de me renvoyer un placet qui vous a été présente par le nom Abraham Schouabe Juif de Metz âge de vingt-deux ans, que j'ai arrêté et conduit au prison du grand Châtelet de l'ordre du Roy, pour avoir fait une friponnerie à la nommée Le Fevre Marchande lingère, cette femme ayant eu besoin d'une somme de huit cents livres, elle eut le malheur de tomber entre les mains de ce juif, cette lingère luy donna pour sureté des huit cents livres, pour deux milles tant délivrés de toiles et de mousselines, cette femme envron au bout d'un an porta les huit cent livres, et soixante livres d'intérêt à ce juif, dans [la] rêvenue de retirer sa toile et mousseline, mais ce juif luy fit entendre qu'il les avait mis engage, et que si elle voulait donner de l'argent qu'il les font retirer, et qu'il luy porterait ses toiles, cette femme ne voulait pas luy donner l'argent qu'en retirant ses marchandises, ce juif, fit si bien en sorte qu'elle eut la facilite de luy confier cinq cents livres elle n'a pas pu retirer cet argent ny ses marchandises, c'est vrai effort pour mieux dire un fripon qui ne fait autre métier que de courir les jeux de Paris et bordelles et d'attraper qui il peut.*" AB, MS 11072, 4-5.

29 This is the first reference to Nathan of Morhange, transcribed here from the rest of the letter: "*Nathan de Morhange autre juif, le dit Schouabe m'a dit qu'il est vrai qu'il a accepté de cette lingère 17 Avril 1728 pour vue une somme de 960 livres de toile qu'il a payé suivant le reçue qu'il m'a montrée d'elle.*" Ibid., 4.

30 The letters continued to focus on Morhange and his relationship to Abraham, transcribed here: "*J'ai parlé à ce juif ce matin qui m'a dit n'avoir jamais prêté d'argent a cette lingère par conséquent qu'il n'a rien les cent soixante livres d'intérêts ni 2853 de marchandises en manifestement, et qu'en un mot pria rien d'elle, ce sont des friponneries dont elle servit plusieurs fois Nathan de Morhange autre juif, le dit Schouabe m'a dit qu'il est vrai qu'il a accepté de cette lingère 17 Avril 1728 pour vue une somme de 960 livres de toile qu'il a payé suivant le reçue qu'il m'a montrée d'elle. J'ose vous assurer Monsieur, avec vérité que ce jeune homme est un vrai fripon, coureur de bordelle, de jeux et cabaret, et que cette lingère est fort à plaindre ce 28 septembre 1729 (7tembre).*" Ibid., 4-5.

31 "Sometime in the spring of 1739, Merle, wife for thirty years of Joseph Worms, died. On 2 December 1739 the Lieutenant-General of the bailliage court of Metz upheld Merle's will. Joseph Worms was deprived of his wife's property as well as the guardianship of his children. Somehow, at least according to Joseph Worms, the rabbi had been silenced and he, Worms, was left without support from the community. His cause was unique, Worms declared, and had never been

tested in any jurisdiction. Can a Jewish woman, in eighteenth-century France living with her husband, disinherit her husband, and deprive him of his guardianship? Can an ordinance from the Lieutenant-General upholding this behaviour be sustained? Merle had apparently wished to leave Worms years before, but her father had persuaded her to remain with her husband. Her father was now dead, and her eldest brother Orly headed the family." Malino, "Resistance and Rebellion," 61.

32 AB, MS 11072, 4-5.

33 Ibid., 15. The testimony was from Abraham himself (spelled Schwab here).

34 Ibid.

35 The release form is transcribed here:

M. Rossingnol
19 Aout
Mémoire
Pour: Abraham Schwabe juif âgé 22 ans
Contre: La nomme la Fevre lingère
Monseigneur
Schwabe fut arrêté 29 septembre et constitué prisonnier à la prison du grand Châtelet ou il est encore actuellement en vertu d'un ordre du Roy plus de 10 mois le sont écouler sans savoir les causes de son emprisonnement, et ce n'est que par l'interrogatoire qu'il a subi le douze du premier moitie d'aout de cette année 1730 par demain Monsieur de Farcey Conseilleur qu'il a découvert que la nommée Le Fevre a occasionne sa détention sous de faux supposes et par des artifices qui mérite répréhensions Elle prétend contre toute vérité avoir confié Schwabe une somme the 500» cette prétendue confiance ne pas pour sous la terre ne s'étant connus de tous les jeux que pour avoir faire une seule négociation de laquelle elle luy a donné une quittance servant de décharge. Dans le fait le 16 aout 1728, La dame Le Fevre envoya dès le suppliant sa servante pour lui dire de venir parler a sa maitresse, il se rendu chez elle sur le champ. Elle luy proposa a vue empreint de 1000 » dont elle disait avoir besoin pour faire un payement, de laquelle somme elle promettait un gros intérêt. Shwabe refusa le prêt n'en ayant jamais fait surcharges, il luy proposa d'acheter ses marchandises qu'il promit payer comptant, elle lui répondit qu'elle n'en avait pour le lendemain, 17 aout, mois d'aout elle luy dit avoir prise face le prie de 1300 » il en examina la facture et suivant l'addition qu'il en fait, elle se retrouverait monter a 900 » qu'il luy offrir. Mais sur la représentation qu'elle l qu'elle avait besoin de 1000 » et que cette marchandise de toile luy coutais 1300 » il luy convient a 960 » qu'lui paye en 40 Louis d'or. Chacun en confiance duquel payment elle luy donna une quittance générale convient les en terminer. Ibid., 23-4.

36 Ibid., 24.

37 Samuel Cahen, *Archives Israélites de France, Revue Mensuelle: Historique, Biographique, Bibliographique et Littéraire*, vol. 1 (Paris: 1840), www.bibliotheque-numerique-aiu.org/idviewer/19220/4.

38 Paris, Archives Nationales (AN), LL 1642.

39 Kahn, *Juifs de Paris*, 126.

40 "*Est-ce que c'est la mutine contre la volonté paternelle?*"; "*Pourquoi elle veut rompre les liens les plus sacrés?*"; "*A quoi bon une protestation qu'eut étouffée un ordre du roi?*" Ibid., 126-129.

41 "*L'autre établissement, celui des* Nouvelles Catholiques, *était situé rue Ste-Anne Ony admettait les femmes hérétiques, moyennant deux cents livres de pension que le roi prenait à sa charge. Les Filles de Nouvelles Catholiques, ne s'occupaient seulement de salut des Juives. Elles s'intéressaient aussi aux juifs, a leurs sentiments religieux et secondaient leur conversion.*" Ibid., 117. The other establishment was that of the *Nouvelles Catholiques*, located at rue Ste-Anne Ony. They admitted women heretics for an average of 200 pounds, which the king usually paid. The institution was particularly focused on religious education and the conversion of Jewish women.

42 The files that are left from the convent of the *Nouvelles Catholiques* are found in the Archives Nationales: LL 1642, the pensioner book; LL 1641, an edition of the constitutions from 1707; LL 1048, financial documents and contracts; H5 4157-4158, *recettes et dépenses*, 1760, 1770, 1781-1782; and H/5/4206, *rentes XVI*[e]*-XVIII*[e]. 1675 edition of the constitutions at Richelieu, Bibliothèque Nationale de France, MS 11766.

43 "*Des juifs de Paris qui allèrent au christianisme les uns ne virent là qu'un moyen d'améliorer leur sort, les autres, cédant à des suggestions pressantes, un moyen de vaincre les préjugés et de s'imposer à une société qui, dans son ensemble, les rejetait loin d'elle.*" Kahn, *Juifs de Paris*, 122. Translation: "The Jews of Paris that went towards Christianity were the ones that wanted to better their lives, others gave in to the pressure of oppression and prejudice that was imposed on them from a society that was so different to their own."

44 The record states that "she entered the *Nouvelles Catholiques* community on 27 October 1729 at the age of eighteen or nineteen." AN, LL 1642.

45 "*Elle y avait été attiré d'abord, disait-elle, par les discours que différents catholiques et même des prêtres avaient tenus devant elle, et poussaient définitivement dans cette voie par les vérités éclatantes que M. Valerot, vicaire de la paroisse de St. Jean et chargé de son éducation religieuse, avait fait briller à ses yeux.*" *Juifs de Paris*, 125-126.

46 "*C'est une demoiselle très raisonnable, assez gracieuse de figure et dont l'on rendait bon témoignage.*" Ibid., 125.

47 "*Néanmoins touché de la désolation de cette enfant, de sa détermination désespérée. Elle lui inspira d'autant plus d'intérêt qu'en realité Angélique ne fuyait le 'Juif Anglais' que parce qu'elle soupirait pour 'un catholique' qui ne la voulait l'épouser qu'elle ne fut baptisée. ...on lui fit signer un engagement en bonne forme qu'elle performa en hébreu et en français: 'Je soussigne, ay de ma pure et propre volonté, sans y ester contrainte par aucune vue humaine, mais par un vray desir d'embrasser la Religion Chrétienne, fait a ce sujet présenter un placet a monsieur le lieutenant de police, en foy de quoy j'ai signé la présente protestation pour y être attachée, fait a Paris le 29 séptembre 1729.*'" Ibid., 125.

48 Ibid. This is a letter/summary from Cardinal de Fleury. He was acting here as conduit to the king.

49 Transcription of the original French by Haley Bowen: "*après sestre sagement conduite icy et y avoir reçue les sacremens de penitence de confirmation et de la l'eucharistie* [sic]." In her in-progress PhD dissertation at the University of Michigan, "Breaching the Cloister: Laywomen, Convents, and the State in the Early Modern French Empire," Bowen examines how laywomen in Paris and New France engaged with the convent as an ambiguous space of both incarceration and spiritual retreat. This community of the Couvent de la Providence went under a few different names, including the Couvent de la Providence du faubourg Saint-Marcel, Filles de la Providence de Dieu, or Hospitalières de la Providence, rue de l'Arbalète. It existed roughly between 1639-1790. Information and translation here are courtesy of Bowen. See documents AN, LL 1062, 1702, 1703, and 1704.

50 Biver and Biver document this in *Abbayes, monastères, couvents*, 313.

51 According to Haley Bowen: "Perhaps she donated to the Couvent de la Providence after arriving there, it would be worthwhile pursuing this line of research in the future...There seems to be no reference to her name. Compared to most other convents in Paris, the surviving archival material on the Nouvelles Catholiques is rather rich in its size. The most helpful document might be the provisional Constitutions written for the community in 1707, which give a sense of what daily life might have been like there in the first half of the eighteenth century (AN, LL 1641). To trace her at this next institution Couvent de la Providence in Paris, to see if she entered as a student, free pensioner, prisoner, or novice." This information derives from a discussion with Haley Bowen about her doctoral research; Bowen has approved its inclusion here.

References

Biver, Paul and Marie Louise Biver. *Abbayes, monastères, couvents de femmes à Paris, des origines à la fin du XVIIIe siècle*. Paris: Presses Universitaires de France, 1975.

Cahen, Samuel. *Archives Israélites de France, Revue Mensuelle: Historique, Biographique, Bibliographique et Littéraire*. Vol. 1. Paris: 1840. www.bibliotheque-numerique-aiu.org/idviewer/19220/4

Geneanet. "Gluck "Angélique" Schwab." Accessed 24 May 2023. https://gw.geneanet.org/alanguggenheim?lang=en&n=schwab&oc=0&p=gluck+angelique

Hertzberg, Arthur. *The French Enlightenment and the Jews*. New York: Columbia University Press, 1968.

Kahn, Leon. *Les Juifs de Paris au Dix-Huitième Siècle : d'après les archives de la lieutenance générale de la police à la Bastille*. Paris: Darlucher, 1894.

Malino, Frances. "Resistance and Rebellion in Eighteenth-Century France." *Jewish Historical Studies* 30 (1987): 55–70.

Conclusion

The documents that record the lives of women in eighteenth-century France provide the materials for a new consideration of the literary genre of forensic storytelling. The metamorphosis of literary tradition from historical testimony to fictitious storytelling owes much to oral tradition and the beginnings of print journalism. The stories embedded in many epistolary novels and the *Causes Célèbres* come from the many briefs and legal documents dictated to scribes and lawyers. Those involved in these cases, principally women, became the subjects of the *Causes Célèbres* and other forms of printed legal literature, which were notorious and popular among the public. In many respects, even the legal factums were false, as they represented a form of storytelling; though rooted in real-life experience, they were themselves fictionalized literary products. The stories recounted in novels were recorded, distorted, and disseminated. This trend anticipated the proliferation of "fake news" and has disturbing and dangerous consequences. Sensationalized tales hold a cautionary note that resonates in our own times. The literary-legal matrix is often in delicate balance. For these reasons, the forensic and material tools used in this study (namely the legal briefs and their contents) help us gain a greater understanding of the complex, culturally situated contexts of historical people's lives.

By using authentic documents, we can derive a deeper meaning and a fuller understanding of the past and of the truth. These are the tools that help us define the history of feminism more clearly. We can see that women exercised what agency they had at their disposal and that they had to be creative and strategic when

DOI: 10.4324/9780429001147-7

challenging authority. The material contents of the legal briefs help us understand the depths of any prisoner's life in greater detail. Though subjects of confinement were often deprived of pen and paper, they sometimes found means of recording their own words and thus communicating with the outside world.

The factum (or legal brief) served as an important way for the public to read fictionalized versions of current events. At the same time, it exposed women's stories to the public in a manner that put them at the mercy of societal scrutiny and left them vulnerable to misogynistic judgment. The factum's status as popular literature provided private and public access to these stories simultaneously. There is a relaxed nature to the epistolary form that appealed to the public and especially women. Through letters, women often figured out how to straddle these spheres by networking and writing so as to be seen and heard.

By reading the file of Marie-Madeleine Bonafon through a feminist lens, we can appreciate the courage it must have taken to challenge the royal court as she did. She demonstrated mastery of the belletristic form through the strategic letters she wrote from confinement. We would do well to appreciate the considerable volume and scope of Bonafon's body of work, which serves as a testament to her intelligence and her success in regaining a good deal of agency over her life. Bonafon's style, spelling, and penmanship all suggest that she was practiced well above the station of chambermaid.

The materials in Bonafon's factum together with her letters (including her expressions of contrition and justifications of her actions) help us understand the role of women and their experiences of oppression more deeply. Bonafon's *roman-à-clef* and its key enable us to expand our understanding of the literature of the time, and especially the literature produced by women.[1] Taken together, the material objects and missives that make up Bonafon's file illuminate the clandestine circumstances in which she wrote, going so far as to illicitly obtain pen and paper to plead for the restoration of her reputation and her life.

There is an interesting fluctuation between formality and vulgarity in Geneviève de Gravelle's writing. At first, she wished to convey her loyalty to and belonging within the nobility. But soon after receiving her second *lettre de cachet*, Gravelle responded with desperate attempts at self-expression, which were at times crude.

Her writing quality degraded, reflecting the reality of her mistreatment as she mentally unraveled. As a result, her story shows how it feels to be progressively deprived of support. We can see through her letters how her marginalization only intensified over time. The vast, chaotic volume and style of her letters demonstrate that her true recourse was her capacity to move readers emotionally—both then and now.

Previous scholarship has produced many negative commentaries on the style and quality of eighteenth-century women's letter writing, as can be seen in the special critiques of Gravelle's letters. Instead, we ought to wonder what her potential goals could have been. Her experience was that of a woman with little to no social or political agency, living an oppressive life that had been imposed upon her. Her file documents reflect her attempts to empower herself by writing and reacting against her forced confinement. Her writings were as much an outlet for herself as they were an irritant for others. Witnessing Gravelle's descent into instability by way of her own documentation enables our understanding of the desperation and depths of feeling that went into her missives. Her efforts cannot be pushed aside or ignored; her behavior should be treated with compassion. For Gravelle, writing prolifically offered a freedom of self-expression that allowed her to express both her anger and her hope.

When researching women consigned to the convent, the file of Glucka-Angélique Schwab provides much food for thought. When one peruses her file, it first appears to be the case of a Jewish woman forced to convert and live in the convent. This false initial impression proves that a forensic storytelling approach to the casefile can uncover a much fuller story, one that is (hopefully) closer to the truth. Her case provides us with evidence of contemporary women strategically acting to resist patriarchal authority when pushed to their limits. Women transcended religious and traditional forms of patriarchal rule (such as arranged marriage) by strategically taking advantage of opportunities that could offer them alternatives.

This study's analysis of the life of Glucka-Angélique Schwab demonstrates how the patriarchal authority of the king was delegated under rabbinical control in the Jewish community, in a pattern that persisted until the modern age. We cannot know what turns Glucka-Angélique's life might have taken after her conversion or what entrée into French society her conversion might have offered. Would she have remained in the convent, or gone on to marry? Many factors could have contributed to her decisions. Yet unfortunately, the last records we have of Glucka-Angélique report her being visited by the priests who made rounds for those near death. These records indicate that she may have been receiving last rites. At 21 years of age, her life ended in the convent.

The letters discussed throughout this book were written by women from behind the high walls of convents and prisons, and they constitute the core of forensic storytelling. This genre of literature is situated at the intersection of studies in historical, sociological, literary-critical, and feminist perspectives of eighteenth-century France. In addition, the *lettres de cachet*, factum, correspondence, and *mémoires* all provide evidence of the marginalization of women in the eighteenth century. Simultaneously, these documents prove that many women demonstrated a great aptitude for writing, documenting, and networking, actions that allowed them to exercise some degree of autonomy. At the heart of the writing found in these files is a confluence between actual history or lived experience and the embellishment of reality that found its way into popular literature. Taken as a whole, these women's stories exhibit a shared sense of purpose, as each of them wrote in protest of their confinement and in reaction against imposed patriarchal authority. The importance of this study emerges through encountering the actual products and objects in their authentic context. By studying the objects and considering the material connections to the past, we gain greater insight into the lived experience of women's agency and the first stirrings of feminist thought.

Note

1 The allegorical fairytale was a literary form popularized by French women like Mlle de Scudery in the seventeenth century.

Index

Note: Endnotes are indicated by the page number followed by 'n' and the endnote number e.g., 20n1 refers to endnote 1 on page 20.

For Product Safety Concerns and Information please contact our EU representative GPSR@taylorandfrancis.com
Taylor & Francis Verlag GmbH, Kaufingerstraße 24, 80331 München, Germany

www.ingramcontent.com/pod-product-compliance
Lightning Source LLC
Chambersburg PA
CBHW070617310726
48982CB00001B/106